BOOT CAMP PRAYER

JONATHAN FERGUSON

ISBN-13: 978-1514888742

ISBN-10: 1514888742

Contents

Phase Two:
Learning how to Engage the Battle in Prayer

- Understand why it is important to expose demonic ranks, and how it helps in our approach to the battle and perspective of spiritual warfare
- Understand various demonic ranks, what they represent, and much more

Chapter 10: Targets & Core Operations of Demonic Ranks

- Learn three main targets of principalities and powers
- Understand eight cultural agendas of principalities and powers and how they establish strongholds in these areas
- Learn the importance of accurately discerning spiritual conflicts, how they affect the way we war, and much more

Chapter 11: Wrestling Principalities

- Learn basics on how to strategically deal with principalities and powers
- Learn three basic and strategic warfare prayers
- Learn why the prayer of agreement is key in spiritual warfare prayers and much more

Chapter 12: Jesus, Our War General

- Realize Jesus's sovereignty in the battle and the importance of submitting to that reality
- Learn why warfare prayers should address God more than they address the enemy
- Learn why it is important to have a battle plan and never engage in war without a clear directive from the Lord and much more

- Review strategic prayers that wrestle down principalities and powers without attracting demonic retaliation
- Understand the power of prayers that shift atmospheres and the importance of discerning spiritual climates and terrains in battle
- Review truths that are important to remember as you advance in the battle and more

- Understand why strategic action must follow strategic warfare prayer
- Understand our mandate to advance the kingdom and more

- Understand the 3 primary ways that answers come in prayer
- Review how to discern when the answer is released in prayer
- Review more on how to overcome feelings of apathy, dryness, and resistance in prayer and more

- Worship Warrior Prayers
- Prayers for God to fight our battles
- Prayers that expose and reverse the strategies of the enemy
- Prayers that vex demons
- Prayers that shift atmospheres and more

Introduction

I believe the Lord mandated me to format the writing style of this book in a strategic and innovative way in order to appeal to both readers and non-readers alike. Therefore, the first phase of this book is a study guide/workbook. The second phase of this book is written in the traditional style.

I really sense that God wants you to take in a greater volume of truth within a shorter period of time. I sensed that the Church needed a fast-track, intensive, and boot-camp-style prep in prayer. Also, if I had not condensed the book, it would've easily been at least double this size. The only problem with that is everyone does not have that kind of attention span.

Because of the demand and mandate to train you for high-level impact in prayer, the Spirit of God led me to compile information in ways that you can study in depth on the subject of prayer without having to dig through any unnecessary preliminaries. The fact is that God is going to use this book to make a warrior out of you. And more specifically, the type of warrior that overcomes the most aggressive satanic oppositions that attempt to prohibit your ability to pray the Kingdom and will of God in the earth.

However, I do not recommend that you exclude any part of this writing because it is very intricate, systemic, and process driven in the way that the truths unfold. This means that if you skip one chapter, you will more than likely not be ready for the following chapter. If you are the type of reader that may skip around from time to time ...

feel free, BUT you will need to be sure that you are eventually embracing the entirety of the message concealed, line-by-line, and precept-by-precept.

And please don't be a person that takes a peek at the following pages and says, "Oh, the first phase is just a lesson outline, so I'm going to skip to the second phase." Although the first seven chapters of this book are more of a study guide, they contain some extremely thorough study material that you cannot afford to miss out on.

There is so much you have to learn in order to become an effective prayer warrior in the first phase of this book. And trust me, I know because I have literally been working on this project for almost ten years trying to strategize on how to compile the years and years of experience and study on prayer. It is without question a groundbreaking equipping tool because it is formatted in this way so that you do not waste any time trying to piece together the many mysteries of prayer.

Basically, in phase one, you will learn multiple principles of cultivating a prayer life that is both effective and intense (James 5:15-18). In phase two of this book, you will learn principles of how to engage spiritual battle in prayer. Ultimately, by the time you complete this book, you will have embraced life-altering truths pertaining to establishing a powerful prayer life.

I can assure you that this book is not, and I repeat, is *not* a book that you merely read and afterwards place on the shelf to collect dust. With your Bible handy, this is a study and reference tool that you will be able to refer to for the rest of your life. And with all of that being said, I want to welcome you to *Boot Camp Prayer*. Now let's get started.

Chapter 1

Developing Commitment in Prayer

Lesson Objectives:
- Review four keys in developing excitement & commitment in prayer
- Review eight powerful things that take place when you pray even when you feel inadequate in your ability to pray
- Review basic principles that you can begin to apply in your prayers immediately and begin to see results and much more

Commitment to Prayer

Pentecost would not exist in America if it were not for a people who had given themselves to prayer prior to the Azusa movement.

Facts About Commitment to Prayer

- Matthew 6:5-7 says, "When", not "if" we pray. Selah. Therefore, Matthew 6:5-7 = prayer is not an option.
- 1 Samuel 12:23 shows prayerlessness is sin.
- Matthew 6:5-7 & Matthew 7:26 teach it's spiritually stupid not to pray.

Jonathan Ferguson

The Proof of Commitment is Consistency

Matthew 7:7- Ask, Seek, and Knock

- Ask and Seek: Understand that Jesus is speaking to His disciples about prayer from a cultural background in which both the words "ask and seek" have same definition in the Hebraic tongue.

- In other words, we have not asked until we seek, and we have not sought until we knock. Therefore, the scripture is saying, "ask and keep asking; seek and keep seeking; knock and don't stop knocking until the door is opened."

- Ask, Seek, Knock, and it shall be opened = whatever has been closed must open up to us when we commit to prayer.

4 Keys in Developing Commitment in Prayer

1.) The 1st key to develop commitment is to "schedule the time"

- Psalm 5:3 -- "Direct prayer" = arrange, set in order.

- The only way to arrange or set your prayer life in order is to schedule a time.

- We schedule everything else, so why not prayer? 1 Samuel 2:30.

Set Time vs. Amount of Time:

Scheduling a time is not always about praying at a particular set time every time you pray. Sometimes

4

scheduling a time is about making sure we accomplish a certain amount of time whenever we pray.

Jesus didn't pray at the same time every day:

- He prayed early morning (Mark 1:35).
- He prayed multiple times a day (Daniel and David accomplished this as well) (Luke 4:42).
- He would withdraw from business to pray (Luke 5:16).
- He spent all night in prayer (Luke 6:12).
- He prayed spontaneously in times of temptation/testing (Luke 22:40-46).

The key is to remain spontaneous and instant in prayer while making sure there is some type of commitment, whether it is a specific appointed time of prayer every day, or a set amount of time that you pray on a daily basis.

2.) The 2nd key to develop commitment is to "Pray Always": (Luke 18:1; 1 Timothy 2:8)

- No matter how spiritual we get or think we are, every day we wake up, our flesh is not going to want to pray.

- Likewise, there is a discipline we must develop to keep our flesh on the altar. Sometimes we will have to treat ourselves as the priests would treat the sacrifice and TIE OURSELVES TO THE ALTAR according to Psalm 118:27 (in a figurative sense).

3.) The 3rd key to develop commitment is to "Pray About Everything": (Philippians 4:6)

- Sometimes PRAYER IS THE ANSWER. It is one thing

to pray for an answer and another thing to understand that prayer is the answer.

- Even when we don't feel like we know how or what to pray for, there are promises and benefits released when we JUST PRAY ANYWAY. In other words, there are some things that prayer accomplishes for us, even when it seems as if we have not accomplished anything in prayer.

When prayer is the answer, it accomplishes the following (See letters a-h):

a) Prayer Helps us Fight Temptation

- Keeps the enemy from taking advantage of us (Luke 22:40,46; Matt 26:35,41).
- Shows us the way of escape (1 Corinthians 10:13).
- Causes us to avoid temptation all together (Matthew 6:13).

b) Prayer Uproots Demonic Systems (Mark 9:29; 2 Corinthians 10:3).

c) Prayer Prepares Us:

- Reveals purpose (Luke 4:42-43; Acts 10:9-20).
- We access wisdom for decisions, and we have a sense of direction (Luke 6:12-13).
- We develop sensitivity to the Holy Spirit (John 5:19).
- We are strengthened in trials (Matthew 26:35-41).

d) Prayer Brings Empowerment (Acts 1:13-14, 2:1-4; Luke 4:14)

Note:
The early church went from power in Acts 2:1-4 (see also Acts 1:8) to "great power" in Acts 4:31-33. They were filled while they prayed in Acts 2, and they were filled again as they prayed in Acts 4. And notice in Acts 4 they were not praying to be filled, but as they were praying one thing, God did more than what they asked.

e) Prayer hides us and keeps us in humility

- Hiding = Psalm 32:7 Preserves us from trouble
- Hiding = James 4:10; 1 Pet 5:6 Positions us to be exalted
- Hiding = John 6:2,15 as follows:

    – Prayer keeps us and puts us back on the right track after success.

    – Prayer keeps us in the right mindset after a success to remember that it was all God.

    Note:
    It's how we pray "after" we're blessed that determines what we're able to handle continually.

    The following scriptures show how Jesus maintained a powerful prayer life even during the height of His ministry success:

    * Matthew 14:23; Luke 5:15,16 (departing to a wilderness)
    * Mark 1:34,35 (before day)
    * Luke 9:10 (with disciples)

7

f) Prayer brings death to the flesh (Rom 6:7,11,12)

Luke 4:2-4 – Notice that Jesus was still denying food after He had already completed the forty-day fast (and yet He still chose to keep His flesh under control).

- Death to earthly things: Colossians 3:1-3; John 3:28-30 (we decrease)
- Death to sin: 1 Peter 4:1-2
- Prayer will break habits and cycles of sin (Matthew 6:13).

g) Prayer strengthens our inner man

A great avenue for this is prayer in the Holy Ghost. See Ephesians 3:16 & 1 Corinthians 14:4. Also see chapter one in my book entitled *Experiencing God in the Supernatural Newly Revised: Prophetic Acceleration.*

h) Prayer brings the manifestation of God's glory (2 Chronicles 7:1, 5:13-14)

The 4th and Last Key in Developing Commitment in Prayer is as Follows:

4.) Continue to develop a powerful prayer life

Scriptures teach us what and how to pray for what we're praying.

As we take the journey of developing a powerful prayer life, there are some Automatic Prayer

Focuses we can learn in the Lord's Prayer Model featured in Matthew 6:10 *(note: Matthew 6:10 features prayer principles, not a prayer formula).*

The Lord's Prayer Model

a.) Our Father + Hallowed be thy name

> *Note: Hallowed= Honor = Praise and worship (Proverbs 3:6)*

b.) Thy Kingdom Come, Thy Will be done:

- Focus on God's agenda first and seek His will.

- Pray the Word of God + Pray prophetic revelation.

Four specifics on God's agenda that we are to continually pray for as follows:

- Israel (Psalm 25:22, 28:9)
- The Church (There are many Apostolic Prayers found in the Epistles) – Ephesians 6:18
- Nations (those in rule) – 1 Timothy 2:1-4
- Harvest and Laborers (Souls) – Matthew 9:38; 1 Timothy 2:1-4

c.) Daily bread: Pray for basic needs.

d.) Ask for forgiveness. Confess your Sins.

e.) Deliver us from evil: Prayers for Protection and Victory

f.) AMEN: Praise and Declarations

- Amen = so be it, it is so, I agree, done...

- Amen is not merely an ending of a prayer, but an announcement that the thing we prayed for is "already done".

The conclusion of the matter is simple: PRAY. I don't care if when you pray you are mixing the Lord's prayer with the pledge of allegiance. Prayer is so powerful that God is able to help you eventually work out the kinks. Until then— PRAY.

Chapter 2

Increasing Effectiveness in Prayer

Lesson Objectives:
- Review why it is important to become both effective and intense in the way we pray
- Review three keys in increasing effectiveness in prayer
- Review the importance of broadening concepts of prayer and becoming more flexible in our prayer practices
- Review the importance of allowing the Spirit of God to navigate your prayer life.

The Effectual & Fervent Prayer

James 5:15-18 — Effectual and Fervent

- Effectual = effective
- Fervent = intense

We need to be both effective and intense in prayer or our prayers will not avail much. It's not enough to have one without the other. The two elements must be combined. We won't see maximum results of intensity in prayer until we become more effective in the way we pray. And we won't be as effective in prayer until we add intensity in the way we pray.

If we don't get the results we desire in prayer, it is because we don't know how to pray in the way to get the results we desire. And the majority of the time, it is because the level of intensity or the level of effectiveness we pray in does not match the level of manifestation we want to see.

As we embrace this revelation and become more skilled in the art of prayer, we begin to understand what level of effectiveness or intensity we are praying in, and what results to expect when praying in a particular type of prayer. With this in mind, let's examine how to increase our effectiveness in prayer and the specific levels of effectiveness we can actually engage in prayer. Afterwards, we will deal with various levels of fervency or intensity in prayer and how to increase them as well.

Three Keys in Increasing Effectiveness in Prayer

#1 One of the first steps in becoming more effective in prayer is to realize that "we don't know how to pray".

- Romans 8:26-27 – We do not know how to pray as we should. Period.

- The more we keep Romans 8:26-27 in mind, the further we will go. We can't get to a place where we assume that we know everything there is to know about prayer.

- Remaining teachable is everything (Matthew 6:10 "Lord, teach us").

In, Matthew 6:10, notice how the original disciples were men whose culture taught them how to pray. The patriarchal system of their day included intensive study on subjects such as prayer and other scriptural foundations. But despite all prior knowledge and experience concerning prayer, the disciples had enough wisdom and humility to understand that they yet needed Jesus to teach them how to pray.

2 Hindrances to Praying More Effectively (See a & b)

a. Assuming that you already know (especially after only seeing little results).

In reality, many pray in ways they have heard others pray and not based on scriptural principles. The problem is that when prayer becomes more ritualistic, it becomes less effective. We must become and remain teachable in order to become and remain effective.

b. Allowing personal desires and pressures to force you into praying amiss.

James 4:3 – praying amiss = praying the wrong thing at the wrong time

Asking Wisdom

James 1:5 and James 4:2-3 give us great wisdom concerning how to pray in times of a crisis. Therefore, many times a crisis comes, and because we don't pray the way the scriptures tell us to pray in crisis, we don't see results. The truth is that when you are in a problem, it is not the best time to pray to get out of the problem, but rather the best time to pray for wisdom according to James 1:5.

However, this does not mean that praying to get out of a problem is a sin. It just means that praying for wisdom in the problem is better. God can rescue us out of a situation if we pray, but He can also prevent us from ever getting in the situation that we were never supposed to be in if we pray as well.

Example:

Job 8:5 – praying "betimes"
- Betimes = before time

Note: The best time to pray to get out of a crisis is before you get in a crisis. There are times when trouble can not be avoided, but many end up in trouble that they could have avoided if they would have simply strengthened their prayer lives from the beginning or betimes (Job 8:5).

#2 The second key in increasing your effectiveness in prayer is to broaden your understanding of prayer (Ephesians 6:18). Both the way we understand prayer and the way we pray must change.

- Ephesians 6:18 speaks of ALL PRYAER. All prayer = All manners and types of praying

- Ephesians 6:18 = there are DIFFERENT type of PRAYERS that get DIFFERENT types of RESULTS.

Scriptures Teach More About Prayer Than Asking and Receiving

- Becoming diverse in your understanding of prayer will help you become holistic in your practice of prayer as well.

- I researched the words *pray*, *prayed*, and *praying* and discovered at least eleven different Hebraic words that define prayer, which is proof that there are many different types of prayers.

The following references are examples of the different aspects of prayer taught throughout scripture:

- Jesus taught: Asking (Luke 11:10), agreement (Matt 18:18-20), binding, and loosing.

- Job taught: Decreeing and declaring (Job 22:27-28)

- Ezekiel and Jeremiah taught: Weeping and wailing

- James taught: Effectual and fervent (James 5:17)

- Paul taught: Praying in the Spirit (1 Corinthians 14:2,7,14), travailing in prayer (Galatians 4:19), groaning in prayer (Romans 8:22-26), birthing in prayer (Galatians 4:19), laboring in prayer (Colossians 4:12), intercession (1 Timothy 2:1), and thanksgiving (Philippians 4:6; 1 Timothy 2:1)

Recap:

- All prayer (Ephesians 6:18) = being diverse in understanding prayer and being flexible in your practice of prayer.

- We don't always engage in prayer the same way.

Sometimes:

Jonathan Ferguson

- We pray to make requests known.
- We pray to hear God.
- We pray to worship.
- We pray to come against demonic powers.

Examples of Diverse Expressions of Prayer:

• When Moses prayed, he beseeched God (Exodus 33:18).

• When Moses prayed, he talked face-to-face, as a man talks to his friend (Exodus 33:11).

• When Moses prayed, he spoke with God mouth to mouth (Numbers 12:8).

• When Jesus prayed, He lifted His voice with strong supplications (Hebrews 5:7).

(Note: This is why in Acts when the early Church prayed, they lifted up their voices. You must understand they were praying with Apostles who had prayed with Jesus; therefore, it was only natural for them to pray like "He" prayed.)

• Elijah prayed earnestly to God (James 5:16-17).

• (2 Kings 4:35) When Elisha prayed, he would pace the floor (2 Kings 4:35).

• Throughout the books of Psalms, when David prayed, he sang and prophesied (speaking to mountains; Mark 11:23).

• At other times, David would be still and just know God (Psalms 46:10). *Note: That's why when Isaiah prayed, he would at times just wait on the Lord and allow Him to renew his strength (Isaiah 40:31).*

16

Relevance:
The more we learn to utilize many scriptural aspects of what prayer consists of in its fullness, the more effective we will become in prayer.

The Key is to Become Versatile (Ephesians 6:18)

- All prayer (Ephesians 6:18) demands we embrace greater understanding. It also allows us to embrace the power and principle of multiple types of prayer.

- Prayer is an art, meaning it has many different unique facets.

Remember:
- All prayer = Different types of prayer with different results.

- This means that in dealing with the effectual and fervent prayer, there are different levels of effectiveness and different levels of intensity that we can learn to pray into.

    YOUR ASSIGNMENT:

    Research Hebraic definitions of the words *pray*, *prayed*, and *praying*. Research different types of prayers, what they are modernly known as, and how they are practiced.

Three Keys in Increasing Effectiveness in Prayer

Continued...

#3 The third key in increasing effectiveness in prayer is to allow the Holy Ghost to navigate your prayer life.

- Romans 8:26-27 – The Holy Ghost makes intercession.

- The most effective prayer is to pray whatever, however, and whenever the Holy Ghost is praying.

Both broadening our understanding of prayer and allowing the Holy Ghost to navigate are equally important:

a. If we don't broaden our understanding in prayer, we are more likely to either fail to recognize or resist how the Holy Spirit may attempt to navigate us through various unfamiliar avenues of prayer.

b. If we don't allow the Holy Spirit to navigate our prayer, as a result, everything we learn about prayer remains useless.

According to Ephesians 6:18, Scripture doesn't leave us in Romans 8:26 not knowing how to pray. In fact, in comparing Romans 8:26 and Ephesians 6:18, the Scriptures acknowledge both our inability to pray and our need to broaden our understanding and practice of prayer. Therefore, according to Scripture, we are to realize that the Holy Ghost is always both praying through us *and* teaching us how to pray.

The more diverse we become our understanding of prayer, the more ready and flexible we are to shift with the leading of Holy Spirit in prayer. The more we allow the Holy Ghost to navigate in prayer, the more He will quicken and empower the knowledge we have embraced about prayer. They both go hand in hand.

As we broaden our understanding of prayer, we learn so many principles of HOW and WHAT to pray. There are many different types of prayers that we begin to learn to function in, such as silence, travail, supplication, and much more.

However, I reiterate, we must yet remain sensitive to the Holy Spirit concerning WHEN we should incorporate WHAT we have learned. If we learn all the types of prayer, but do not allow the Spirit of God to navigate, it can defeat the purpose. The Spirit of God must navigate WHEN we are to travail, WHEN we are to be silent, or WHEN we are to ask and seek, etc.

It is very possible to travail, ask, seek, supplicate, and attempt to utilize as many prayer principles as we like with no power and to no results. Our prayers must always be directed by the Holy Ghost (Psalms 80:18). Prayer is only powerful when God's Spirit is in it, quickening it to life.

Three Basic Things Happen When He Quickens Prayer (Psalms 80:18)

- Prayer becomes easy and even enjoyable.
- The life of the Holy Ghost fills the very words we speak.
- Prayer becomes powerful and brings about results.

NOTE: You will learn more about Holy-Ghost-powered prayer later. For now, the previous list will suffice as a foundation. However, as it pertains to becoming more effective in prayer, allowing the Holy Ghost to navigate your prayer life is of utmost importance. Everything we learn of prayer has to be submitted to how He chooses to lead us in prayer; otherwise, our prayers will not avail much.

And now that you understand how to become more effective in prayer, I want to take the next chapter to go deeper. Let's examine specific levels of effectiveness in prayer and other lost arts of prayer that I have discovered and seen many results in my journey. In doing so, I believe you will gain great clarity in what it means to become more effective in prayer.

Chapter 3

Five Levels of Effectiveness in Prayer

Lesson Objectives:
- Review five levels of effectiveness in prayer.
- Review what it means to pray strategically.
- Review the work of the Holy Ghost in prayer and eight benefits that come along with it.
- Review keys that will help you pray under the unction, power, and direction of the Holy Spirit.
- Review two lost and powerful arts of prayer.
- Review more than fifteen benefits of waiting on the Lord in prayer, and much more.

I don't want you to merely read about becoming more effective in prayer in a vague way, but I want you to dig deeper with me. In this chapter, we'll examine specific levels of effectiveness in prayer and what they are.

I have discovered that the scriptures are very specific concerning activities that are effective in prayer and produce certain results. This is what I mean by *levels* of effectiveness in prayer.

As you read, you will locate where you are in your prayer life. You will understand why you have been getting the results you have been getting in prayer, and what you can do to increase your effectiveness and see more of the results you would like to see.

You will review various scriptural secrets of the Holy Spirit's work in prayer and what I like to call "lost arts of prayer." Actually, the secrets and the arts go hand in hand.

The lost arts are in fact maneuvers in prayer that can be utilized in helping us cooperate with the work of the Holy Ghost in our prayers. And although these secrets are found in scripture, we often do not acknowledge or utilize the power of their principles in our personal prayer settings.

These technologies of prayer are often dismissed or altogether not considered to be in any correlation with prayer at all, which is why I refer to them a lost arts. We will explore them, but let's first examine *5 Levels of Effectiveness in Prayer*.

5 Levels of Effectiveness in Prayer

1) Making mention (of a person or thing) – Ephesians 1:16

> The revelation lies is the fact that there is not much skill or labor required in this level of prayer. However, when we simply mention things in prayer, the power is that what we mention automatically becomes subject under the canopy of grace that is already established in our prayer lives, whatever level they may be on. Not to mention the eight benefits of "when prayer is the answer" as listed in Chapter 1. Remember, the eight benefits show us how powerful our prayers are, even at a beginner's level. We're also reminded of the results that come into our lives even when we do not feel as though we can pray or our prayers are working (See Chapter 1).

2) Make requests known (write a list) – Philippians 4:6

This level requires that we become more specific in what we desire. However, this scripture only promises that we will receive peace. This means that the only promised results of prayer in this level is that we will have an assurance that everything will be ok. However, there is no guarantee that we will receive what we are asking for. Review the following:

− Receiving peace vs. receiving what we ask (1 John 5:14).

− Remember when we pray on this level, the Bible does not say that we will receive what we petition. It says that we will receive peace. Why? Because only when we pray in the next level of effectiveness, are we guaranteed to receive what we ask.

3) Pray the Word of God − 1 John 5:14

It is only at this point that we are guaranteed to receive exactly what we are asking for. Period.

4) Strategic Prayer

• The previous level of effectiveness in prayer is to pray the promises of God; however, to pray strategically is to, pray the conditions required in order for the promises of God to come into manifestation (I will explain this in detail momentarily).

• Praying strategically is important because there are times when we pray the promises and are guaranteed the result, but the only problem is that the promise cannot come until the condition of the promise is met.

A Brief Word on Praying Strategically

A person who prays strategically understands that for every promise or prophecy from the mouth of God, there is a condition on our part for the promise or prophecy to come to pass. Therefore, in addition to praying the promises of God, they go the extra mile to make sure that the conditions of what God has promised are being met. We will briefly touch on strategic prayer more in the chapter on Binding & Loosing, but for now let's consider one example.

Example:

The scriptures mention how the Lord appeared to Solomon, gave him an opportunity to pray for anything he desired, and promised to grant it. However, Solomon was only granted one request. I'm not going to give you the complete story because I want you to do your homework and research it.

Simply stated, Solomon's request was for wisdom. And when Solomon asked for wisdom, I believe it represented Solomon's keen ability to pray strategically.

Solomon demonstrated to us how to pray strategically, in that he asked for the prerequisite of wealth when he asked for wisdom (Proverbs 3:13-16). In fact, if he had asked for wealth and riches, he wouldn't have gotten wealth, riches, or wisdom.

Solomon understood that wisdom is the condition for wealth and riches. Therefore, instead of praying for wealth, Solomon asked for wisdom because he understood strategically that wealth would also come as a result of possessing wisdom.

Note: Sometimes we ask for the "wrong thing" instead of asking for the "right thing" that will release the "desired thing."

Strategic praying = we become very intentional in the way we pray, meaning we know "what" we are after and we know "how" to go after it.

When you pray strategically, you not only know what to pray for, but you also know how to pray for it and when to pray for it. The opposite of this is to pray amiss. And praying amiss is simply NOT asking for the right thing at the right time, which leads to our final level of effectiveness in prayer.

5 Levels of Effectiveness Continued:

5) Praying in the Spirit – Ephesians 6:18

- Praying in Tongues – 1 Corinthians 14:2, 4, 14 (For in depth teaching on this refer to my book: *Experiencing God in the Supernatural Newly Revised*)

- Praise and Worship – Some things we don't have to ask for while in His presence.

- Allowing the Holy Ghost to navigate your prayers

The way you know you have entered into the highest level of effectiveness in prayer is when you enter into the Spirit. Whether it is through speaking in tongues, spending time in worship, or simply allowing the Holy Ghost to navigate your prayers, it is at this place that you lose control. The goal is that He takes over.

Holy Spirit Empowered Prayer

Now that we have made it to this point, I want you to utilize the following outline in order to examine more closely the work of the Holy Ghost in prayer from the context of Romans 8:26-34. Afterwards, I will introduce two lost arts of prayer that will assist you in cooperating with the work of the Holy Ghost in prayer.

However, as you examine Romans 8, be sure to actually read the scriptures and get them in your spirit and not just go over the outline. The outline will make more sense if you do so.

Romans 8:26-34

Romans 8 shows us at least eight benefits that are available to us when we enter into this dimension of effective praying as follows:

- Vs.26 The Holy Spirit picks up our inability to pray and upgrades our prayer lives
- Vs.28 all things work together
- Vs. 28 and we know all things work = we receive heaven's perspective concerning where we are
- Vs. 29 conformed to His image = our identity changes (Sonship)

- Vs. 30 there is a constant awareness and assurance of our salvation
- Vs. 31 no enemies can stand against us
- Vs. 32 freely gives us all things = we become aware of what is released in prayer
- Vs. 33-39 we are assured of our salvation and victory on Christ

As we can see, Romans 8 is full of mysteries in prayer...

Five Mysteries of Prayer in Romans 8 that bring Insight into the Power of Spirit-led Prayer.

1. Vs. 26 = Real power in prayer is in our inability to pray.

2. Vs. 28 All things work together. Note: This promise is only for people who rely on the Holy Ghost to pray through them according to scriptural context.

3. Vs. 26 The Spirit maketh intercession = Prayers are not answered because "we pray," yet we must pray in order for prayers to be answered. It's not about how good we think we do or do not pray that determines the results, BUT THE FACT THAT THE HOLY GHOST IN US IS PRAYING FOR AND THROUGH US.

4. Vs. 34 "...it is Christ that died..." The power of answered prayer is in the death, burial, resurrection, and ascension of Jesus.

   Note: I will explain this more in just a moment, but for now you only need to know that Romans 8:34 is giving us revelation to why there is power released when we pray in Jesus's name.

Already Done in Jesus's Name

- "In Jesus name" = we understand that everything we need or want is already done and finished at His cross.

The Power of "Already Done":

- Romans 8:32- REMEMBER: "...Freely give us all

things..." is in context of PRAYER, and the DEATH, BURIAL, RESSURECTION.

- 2 Corinthians 1:20- all the promises of God are YES AND AMEN.

Yes & Amen
(2 Corinthians 1:20)

- Before we pray, the answer is already YES.
- When we pray the word of God, we pray the answer, not the request.
- When we say, "Amen," our prayers become a prophecy.
- Amen = so be it; it is so; I agree.
- Amen is not to end prayer but to acknowledge what we prayed for is "already done."

The 5th & Final Basic from Romans 8

5. Vs. 34 – Jesus is making intercession.

Romans 8:34 is *the* mystery of all five mysteries, so pay close attention. If you have been wondering how these five mysteries bring any insight into the power of Spirit-led prayer, you will need to understand this final mystery in order to connect the dots.

You have to understand that the Holy Ghost is making intercession (Roman 8:26) for no other reason, but that Jesus is making intercession (Romans 8:34). And Jesus is making intercession on the basis of His death, burial, resurrection, and ascension.

When we pray in Jesus's name, thanking Him and realizing that everything we need and want already belongs to us because of what He has already done, WE THEN TAP INTO THE POWER OF THE HOLY GHOST IN OUR PRAYER

LIVES. Now we are praying what HE is praying. Jesus is praying, the Holy Ghost is praying, and the most effective prayer is to pray whatever HE is praying.

The Power of Prayer is the Power of His Presence

2 Facts (See a & b):

   a. Romans 8:15 Spirit of Adoption = we cry = prayer power.

   b. 1 Corinthians 2:12 ...we have received...the Spirit...that we might know the things...freely given...

The 1 Corinthians 2:12 + Romans 8:15 Revelation

We don't know what's ours until we're in the Spirit (1 Corinthians 2:12). This also means that we can't claim that anything belongs to us until we are in His presence. Therefore, prayers are only answered in His presence (Isaiah 55:6).

Prayer is only quickened in His presence. And when He quickens prayer, it activates our prayer power, which is a cry of the Spirit to the Father from inside of us (Romans 8:15). Note: Quicken = awaken, make alive, empower

Becoming Sensitive to His Presence in Prayer: Waiting on the Lord

Waiting on the Lord can often consist of a balance of spiritual disciplines that seem contradictory. The scriptures admonish us to be slow to speak as we come into His presence, and yet we are also instructed to be instant in prayer, which has a lot to do with being able to catch the spontaneity of the wind of God in prayer. There are other examples as follows:

- Slow to speak (Ecclesiastes 5:1-2) **VS.** Instant in prayer (Romans 12:12)

- Waiting on the Lord (Isaiah 40:31) **VS.** Stir ourselves and meet Him with rejoicing (Isaiah 64:5, 7)

Where Waiting and Spontaneity Meet

- Wait = Strength (Isaiah 40:31)
- Praise = strength (Nehemiah 8:10)

Note: Both of the previous bring power (strength) and direction in prayer. It is easier to realize how waiting brings direction in prayer, but only by revelation can you understand how praise brings direction in prayer. Let me explain.

How Praise Brings Direction in Prayer:

Psalm 100:4- Enter His "gates" with thanksgiving

- Gates= where elders give counsel and wisdom

Note: I believe this counsel and wisdom at the gates could prophetically represent how in praise we receive the instruction and leading of the Holy Ghost in prayer. This is partly why Jesus taught that as we enter prayer, we should "Hallowed be Thy name"....

Becoming Sensitive to His Presence in Prayer
Continued

There are times in prayer that consist of waiting until we feel prompted to pray. We wait until He literally unctions and gives us what to pray (Psalm 80:18). There are other times where we must stir ourselves and seek the Lord when His presence is seemingly absent.

There are also times when as soon as we simply yield to the work of the Holy Spirit, HE TAKES OVER! All of these are disciplines that we must rely on the Spirit of God to lead us into the balance of as we pray.

As we conclude this thought, I want to deal with multiple scriptural benefits of waiting on the Lord. I also want to deal with benefits of journaling your prayer time with God because I believe that waiting and writing have become two lost arts of prayer that bring about tremendous power in prayer.

Two Lost Arts of Prayer:
(Remember: The following two arts of prayer will assist you in better cooperating with the Holy Ghost in prayer.)

1.) Writing:

- Isaiah 37:14-15
  Writing is received as a prayer.

- Deuteronomy 6:3-12
  Writing reinforces our faith concerning the promises of God. It also helps us remember that it was God that performed in our lives.

Jonathan Ferguson

- Habakkuk 2:2-3
  Writing brings clarity and acceleration.

2.) Waiting:

Psalms 63:1-10
  o Waiting is a sign of seeking Him.
  o Our souls are satisfied with marrow and fatness when we wait.
  o Our souls follow hard when we wait.
  o His right hand upholds us when we wait.
  o Those that seek to destroy us go down and fall by the sword when we wait.

How to wait?
Psalms 63:6- Remember, meditate, & watch

Note: To wait is not to be idle, but to be still and know (Psalm 46:10). If you are "still" yet not "knowing," you are not waiting, and your mind is guaranteed to wander or easily be distracted. In order to wait, we must both become vulnerable and have a certain mentality concerning allowing God to be God:

The Proper Mindset While Waiting

A.) John 15:4,7
- Abiding in Him
- Apart from Him nothing
- He and His Word abide in us

B.) Hebrews 11:6
- Believing that He is and that He's a rewarder

C.) Isaiah 30:15
- Quietness and confidence = strength

D.) 2 Chronicles 16:9
- Know He's always moving (realize it John 5:17)

E.) 1 Peter 5:6
- Humble myself; cast all cares and concerns (James 4:6-10)

F.) Proverbs 25:6; Psalm 80:18
- Getting into a place where we allow Him to quicken and unction everything during our time of prayer

More Benefits of Waiting:

- Renewed strength – Isaiah 40:31

- Purging –John 15:2-11 vs. 2

- Cleansing – John 15:2-11 vs. 2

- Bearing fruit – John 15:2-11 vs. 2, 4, 5, 8

- We ask what we will and it is done – John 15:2-11 (See vs. 7)

- He will raise us up – 1 Peter 5:6-10

- He will quicken our prayer life – Psalms 80:18

- We become aware of His presence – Hebrews 11:6

- He fights our battles – Exodus 14:13-14

- We see His salvation – Exodus 14:13

- He counsels us – Job 29:21; Psalms 106:13

- We become sober and vigilant – 1 Peter 5:6-10

- We build up our strength to resist – 1 Peter 5:6-10 / James 4:6-10

5 Levels of Effective Prayer Conclusion

Once you have developed in prayer and begin to pray with more effectiveness, the only way to become most effective in prayer is to add intensity. And once you marry effective prayer with fervent prayer, you will begin to see your prayers avail much as James 5:15-18 promise. For this reason, the next couple of chapters will examine how to increase your intensity in prayer so that it matches that level of effectiveness you pray into.

Chapter 4

Fervent Prayer

Lesson Objectives:
- Learn what it means to pray fervently.
- Review four types of prayers that have great intensity.
- Understand the scriptural significance of praying with intensity.

What is Fervent Prayer?

In addition to learning what it means to be effective in prayer, and different levels of effectiveness in prayer, we should remember that there are different levels of intensity in prayer as well (James 5:15-18). This is what fervent prayer is all about.

Fervency is the level of intensity, passion, and aggression we seek God with. It is when we direct all of our mind, soul, heart, and strength in the prayer. There is COMPLETE focus. The prayer is heartfelt, passionate, and yes, we are actually striving and laboring.

These are the types of truths that I've designed the next couple of chapters to teach you. I want you to have the type of intensity in prayer that moves mountains and causes the grounds to shake (Mark 11:23-24; Acts 4:31).

Four Types of Fervent Prayers

#1 Supplication:

Supplication is the first type of fervent prayer, and there are many words that can describe this term, but there are only a few words that I want you to think of when you think of supplication (**See a, b, & c**.)

a. Beseech (Exodus 33:18):

> The word beseech is actually one of the definitions for the word supplication, and it means to entreat, beg, urge ... "NOW".
>
> *Note 1:*
> *In context of fervent prayer, begging is not in reference to a lack of believing that the promise already belongs to us, but RATHER THE TONE OF DESPERATION IN OUR PRAYER LIVES.*
>
> *Note 2:*
> *The fact that this word is defined as "now" shows how the very nature of how beseeching God places a demand on heaven, which leads to our next word.*

b. Importunity (Luke 11:8):

> • Importunity is defined as boldness; the root word denotes reverence, modesty, and decency.
>
> • It's bold, yet respectful. Importunity understands that we can't make God do anything, but we can command Him concerning His words (Isaiah 45:11).

- Isaiah 45:11 = Hold Him to His words

- Importunity = REFUSE TO BE DENIED

Example:
1 John 5:14 – God doesn't answer prayer because He hears, but because "WE KNOW HE HEARS."

It's a confidence, similar to when a man loves and pursues a woman although she turns him down—"PERSISTENCE"
- It's a certain attitude we embrace (Luke 11:8).

Note:
In Luke 11:18, the man in the text had a certain attitude. He decided that even if he was to get on his neighbor's last nerve, he was going to get what he was looking for.

*** There are some things that we don't even have to feel like God wants to give us. We just have to understand that as we keep praying we place a demand on God's attention and response to our prayers. ***

c) Earnestly (James 5:17):

- Prayer + earnestly. Both words in James 5:17 originate from same Greek root word.

- Prayer + earnestly = Place of prayer, pray, prayed, praying.

- The revelation of the previous is: We "pray"

for something, and even though we've already "prayed" for it, we keep on "praying" for it. We let nothing move us out of our "place of prayer:"

- Note: Elijah prayed seven times while sending his servant back and forth, and yet remained in his place of prayer.

- Although vain repetitions are not good in prayer, REPETITION can, however, be key in fervent prayer. Many misunderstand this.

- **Vain Repetitions** (Matthew 6:7-8): Nothing is wrong with repetition, but the problem is when the repetition becomes vain.

Repetitions in Prayer:

- Elijah prayed for the same thing seven times.

- Jesus and Paul prayed for the same three times.

What Distinguishes a Vain Repetition?

- Vain repetitions are different than the types of repetition we may pray in the context of fervent prayer, as seen in the book of 1 Kings, which is one of many illustrations of effective repetitious praying.

- Vain repetition = Repetitious "because" I think God doesn't hear + Repetitious because I'm more interested in people hearing and admiring the prayer than God.

- Fervent prayer = I'm Repetitious "because" I know

God hears me

- Rule of thumb: Sometimes we pray one time and move on to thanking God. Other times, we press in and "keep praying." We shouldn't confuse "praying earnestly" with "vain repetitions."

Note: Sometimes repetition is required because we need to pray through in a matter and do so without ceasing (See Ephesians 6:13-14; Hebrews 6:12; 10:36).

How to pray through?

a. Keep praying but with perspective that it's already done. Stand in Faith.
b. Fight thoughts of unbelief, condemnation, and thoughts of maybe having not done something right.
c. Understand we may need to adjust our prayer according to progressive revelation. Remember that there are root causes that hinder prayers; therefore, we need God to show us how to see manifestation of what's already done.

How to Pray Without Ceasing?

- To pray without ceasing is to remain in fellowship with God concerning a matter until there is a solution and an answer.

- However, it is key we understand that praying without ceasing is beyond a labor of prayer and is rather a constant dialogue with the Father. It is similar to how Adam walked with God in the garden of Eden and how Moses had a "mouth to mouth" relationship with the Father, which is the highest place of prayer. Praying without ceasing is more about walking with God like Enoch did, and keeping in constant fellowship with Him so you can hear and obey. You will notice that the more you walk with God, certain breakthroughs in the Spirit being attributed not necessarily to the thing you labored in prayer over but more about the thing that you carried in your spirit as you maintained constant fellowship with the Father.

Earnest Prayer Continued:

Note: More definitions of the word Earnest = a show of deep sincerity and seriousness; a sense of importance or urgency.

Examples of Urgency:

- If a kid was to touch fire or walk across the street
- If your life was in danger

Many are lukewarm in prayer and don't even know it. There is often a lukewarm approach in the sense that they do not reach out to God in prayer with any type of urgency.

Africa Story – Pray or Die

There is a story that I viewed on TBN about a town in Africa that was under an attack with multiple shootings happening in villages throughout the day. Some of the Christians there would go hide in the woods all day and wait until night, just to have an opportunity to pray. They would pray with such urgency because they never knew what day they would lose their lives if God did not help them. Eventually, God intervened because of their prayers, and some of the largest churches in Africa were birthed there.

How would you pray if your life depended on it?

Our Hindrances to Praying Earnestly:

Our need doesn't seem immediate as individuals who may be enduring such circumstances as those in the previous illustration.

- We have too many other options just in case God does not come through. Therefore, prayer is often not our priority.

- Many don't pray fervently until they have no other choice.

Note: Those who pray earnestly understand that we should pray like our lives depended on it, whether our need seems immediate or not.

The Strength of Supplication:
"The Effort"

- Although we do not depend on our works, the strength of supplication is in the effort we put forth in lifting our voices to God in prayer.

- Hebrews 5:7 shows that even Jesus put forth extreme effort in His prayers and that He did so in "STRONG CRYING".

- Hebrews 5:7- Strong crying vs. tears = notice the text doesn't say "weeping" but "crying."

- Strong crying = Jesus was lifting up His voice = this is the "Strength of supplication"

When we:
- Yell
- Shout (roar)
- Scream
- When we Lift our voices and allow the Holy Ghost to breathe a fresh wind behind it, things are shaken, barriers are removed, walls are brought down, demonic powers are broken, etc.

WHY?

It's not only a loud cry, but it's from our innermost being, and because it is from spirit, it is recognized by the Spirit. When we lift our voices in prayer in cooperation with how the Spirit of God is breathing upon us to do so, we resound in the realm of the Spirit in like manner as if God's voice is being heard. We will deal with the power of this from Psalm 29 in more detail in chapter six.

Note: Another definition of supplication is to become weak and cause to suffer.

Example:

Luke 22:44 – Jesus prayed in agony meaning:
- He wasn't praying because He felt the anointing.
- He wasn't praying because He felt like it.
- He wasn't praying because He was getting desired results.

Observation:
When you pray fervently, you pray against all odds, and there's little that can discourage you from praying, and in it, you're willing to become weak and be caused to suffer.

Back to Luke 22:44

Not only did Jesus pray in agony, but He prayed in agony

MORE EARNESTLY. This means that the more uncomfortable He felt, the stronger He prayed.

When we pray with all of our strength, we literally pray until we can't pray anymore because we understand:

- Sacrifice
- The reward of diligent seeking
- The glory revealed in suffering (Romans 8:18)

Things to Note:

- (2 Corinthians 4:17) Affliction is working an exceeding glory.

- Affliction working = there is always a level of friction and discomfort required to produce the glory that God wants to reveal.

Note: At times we underestimate the effort involved. We think if we just "hit at it" and God doesn't bless it, we give up. We have to do it harder, longer, with tenacity, commitment, and relentlessness. It's not as easy as it's advertised. It comes with pain and discomfort at times. When we grossly underestimate the intensity of the effort, we are shocked by the trauma and we run away from the process. – Bishop T.D. Jakes

The Second of Four Types of Fervent Prayer is:

#2 Travail: groaning, birthing

- Travail is a spiritual birthing.

- When our supplications reach a place in which our

personal strength is maxed out, travail is the solution to attain strength in order to continue birthing the prayer out.

- In travail, our prayers take on a Spirit-empowered grown. It is a sound that we can release and a power that is birthed in prayer even beyond words according to Romans 8:26-27.

- Romans 8:26-27 – The Spirit bears our infirmity.

- Infirmity = weakness, pains = the Holy Ghost bears our weakness and pain, and prays through us with His strength.

Observation:

Travail is powerful because of the exchange of strength that takes place as the Holy Ghost prays through us. Our strength maxes out, and then we tap into His strength (2 Corinthians 12:9). After we've prayed until we can't pray anymore, we continue to press in because at this point is where the Holy Ghost causes us to give birth. There are times when we have prayed all we could pray or the burden of prayer is just too heavy. Those are the times when the Holy Ghost steps in so that the intensity of our prayers goes beyond our strength and even our own words (Romans 8:26-27).

Hannah's Vexation is a Great Example of Travail
1 Samuel 1:10,13

- Vs. 10 – This thing vexed her so much that she prayed in the bitterness of her soul, and she wept sore.

- Vs. 13 – Her prayers were so intense that they went beyond words: moaning, sobbing, weeping, wailing, etc.

- Hannah had so tapped in that Eli thought she was drunk (ws.13):

- Note 1: Drunken = Acts 2:15 = Rom 8:26-27 (Holy Ghost) = a groan beyond words = travail.

- Note 2: The word Travail is defined as birth pains= the pain is not killing us; the pain is birthing us

Instead of running from the pain, the pain becomes the drive and fuel we pray with (remember how Jesus prayed in agony more earnestly). Sometimes we don't feel like praying. The sacrifice becomes overwhelming, but that's where we learn how to travail if we continue to press in. Sometimes all we can do is cry, moan, weep, and groan. But whatever we do, we must keep praying because when we get to the place where we can't pray any more, the Holy Ghost will bear our infirmity, and He will begin to pray through us.

#3 Warfare prayer is the third of four types of fervent prayers.

Warfare prayers can include same characteristics of both supplication and travail, yet the intensity of the tone is different. Although the expressions and manifestations are similar, the tone is often indignant, aggressive, or commanding.

Note: A parent can distinguish a child's cry of hurt or anger...

In warfare, we pray in a way to take authority over demonic powers. We pray in order to attack, and we pray to command (Mark 11:23; Job 22:28). Simple things like our attitude, mentality, and tone of voice can distinguish the authority that we pray with; yet we should keep in mind that warfare prayers should be engaged rather with care and proper instruction because it consists of more than lifting our voices and making commands. We will cover in detail warfare prayer within multiple chapters later in the book, but for now we only need to know that warfare is one of the expressions of praying fervently.

#4 Corporate prayer

Corporate prayer is the fourth and final type of fervent prayer. It is so powerful for no other reason than it houses the power of the agreement, and there is so much that you are about to learn of its power.

This is key because now that you understand the importance of praying with intensity and what it means to do so, understanding the power of corporate prayer will be the bridge you cross over in order to begin understanding HOW to actually pray with more intensity.

An Army of Prayer Warriors

In the next chapter, I offer insights on the power of agreement in prayer that happens in a corporate gathering of believers. I really pray that pastors reading this chapter will begin to apply these principles with their congregations because I earnestly believe that God is establishing an army of prayer warriors and intercessors.

I even have a prayer CD also entitled *Book Camp Prayer* available on iTunes, Amazon digital music, and every other digital music platform that exists. The music is genuinely anointed to increase the intensity of prayer for those who listen and pray along. It is also my way of coming into agreement in prayer with people I have never met in person.

Also, one of the reasons that agreement in prayer is essential is because in James 5:13-18, the effectual fervent prayer is actually mentioned in the context of the corporate gathering. In this text, we learn that there were many miraculous things that took place as the early church gathered in prayer. As they prayed, sins were forgiven, sick bodies were healed, and afflictions were subsided.

The text even references how when Elijah prayed with that same intensity, the results were also evident in how the climate of the whole earth was altered for three years(James 5:13-18). God is, yet again, raising a company of people who pray with the intent of seeing such supernatural results in prayer. However, I reiterate that we must become both more effective and more intense in the how we pray if we want our prayers to avail much.

Before you move on:

- Remember: The effectual and fervent prayer is mentioned in context of the corporate gathering. This means that the corporate gathering of prayer is designed to help cultivate in the life of the believer greater intensity and effectiveness in prayer.

- Remember: The corporate gathering of prayer is also designed to create an atmosphere where:

  - Miracles take place (James 5:14).
  - Glory can manifest (Matthew 18:20).
  - Power is made available (James 5:16) .

Chapter 5

How to Increase Intensity in Prayer

Lesson Objectives:
- Review five ways to increase intensity in prayer and much more.
- Understand the power of agreement in prayer/
- Understand the significance of spending more time in prayer.

One of the greatest ways to increase intensity in prayer is to pray in agreement with others. Therefore, I want to first take the time and examine the power of corporate prayer, and afterwards, I will cover four additional ways to increase intensity in prayer.

Understanding the Corporate Anointing:

The corporate anointing is an anointing that is only available when a group of believers gather together. And according to 1 Corinthians 12-14, the corporate anointing is for the purpose of edifying the believer.

To edify literally means to build. This means that the corporate anointing is designed by nature to be one that is building, ever increasing, and not easily broken (see Also Ecclesiastes 4:12). When we are in corporate prayer, the intensity of the prayer is designed to progressively increase exponentially.

Key Notes Concerning Exponential Increase

- Deuteronomy 32:30 – one can chase a thousand and two, ten thousand...

- The Revelation: According to Deuteronomy 32:30, the difference in agreement is exponential.

- Understanding the difference in 2 chasing 2,000 vs. 2 chasing 10,000 is where we begin to understand the science behind an exponential increase of intensity in prayer.

- If one represents a thousand, two representing two thousand would be an increase by addition, but two representing 10,000 is rather an increase by multiplication.

The Overflow of Power:
- Psalm 133:1– Unity is good and pleasant and in it, the anointing flows from "THE HEAD".

- Psalms 23:5 – God anoints "OUR HEADS" for no other reason than to cause our cups to run over.

- The revelation is that there's an "overflow" of power in the corporate anointing.

More Keys Concerning Exponential Increase

- Psalm 34:3 --Magnify the Lord "WITH ME".

- Magnify = to make big

- Whatever the Lord does, no matter how small it seems, we should MAKE IT BIG (Romans 12:15- rejoice with them that rejoice...).

- The objective is that when we celebrate and rejoice together, the anointing builds. In other words, the power in me is multiplied by the power in you, and the results are that there is an overflow.

Three Words that Helps us Understand the Corporate Anointing:
Assembling, Agreement, Accord

1) Assemble:

An Assembly Is:
- The connecting place of multiple parts –one piece to another.
- It's not just coming to church.

Assembling is not about merely coming together, but what we bring to the table. We can come together and still not be assembled. It is not about how many showed up, but how many show up in agreement.

2) Agreement:

- The word agreement comes from the Greek word *symphoneo*, which is where we get our English word symphony.

- A symphony is where multiple instruments play multiple parts in order to produce ONE SOUND.

- Agree = everyone plays their part

- "Forsake not the assembly" = When we come together, we make sure we play our part and bring something to the table. We look for how the power inside of us can connect with the power within another.

  a. More people is not more power, but rather more agreement is more power.

  b. God doesn't count people, He "weighs" them; (Proverbs 16:2)= He wants to know how HEAVY we are in the anointing, not how many people we can pack in a room.

  c. Gideon had too many = When God finds agreement, even if just two or three, they become the majority vote in the Spirit. The power of agreement in the Spirit is greater than the sway of popular opinion. We will explain this more later.

3) Accord (Acts 2:1):

- Accord = same mind, same voice + One Accord = One mind, one voice

Not only in Acts 2:1, but in Acts 4:24, also; they lifted up their voice with one accord. Not only did they come with the same agenda, but they also prayed with the "same mindset" and "same intensity." On the contrary, at times we are not as effective as the early church when praying together because we are either on different levels in our understanding of how to pray, or we are not willing or able to pray with compatible intensity (Matthew 26:40). However, this book is helping you increase both the levels of effectiveness and intensity that you pray in, so that you will see more results in both your personal and corporate prayer lives.

How to Pray in Agreement

Matthew 18:19-20 – Come together focused on Jesus … this is a big part of what it means to pray in Jesus's name.

When we pray in Jesus's name:
- We come in expectancy.
- We welcome Him in.
- We allow Him to have His way.
- We have access to what we desire in prayer through His presence.
- We share common interests and ground with each other (See Acts 2:1; Luke 24:49-53; Acts 1:14).

How to Tap Into the Corporate Anointing?

Acts 2:1 One Accord = One Mind + One Voice= same expectancy and intensity

Note: It was in this place that they all suddenly began to hear, see, and experience the same thing in prayer (See Acts 2:1-4).

How to pray with "One Mind"?

Acts 1:14; Luke 24:49,53 – It was in praise that the Church in the upper room tapped in and began to have the same agenda. They were on the same page. Sometimes we need to add praise and fasting with our prayers in order to increase the agreement. Praise and fasting can be a means of focusing our minds on one agenda and getting on the same page, not only with each other, but also with heaven.

How do we pray with "One Voice"?

A few simple ways to actively agree:
- Holding hands
- Saying Jesus's name
- Praying in tongues
- Praise

Review:
Acts 4:24; Acts 2:1-4

Remember:
Agreement = symphony = every man plays his part

Praying with Intensity Corporately

Note: The key in striving for corporate intensity in prayer is found in Romans 15:30.

Romans 15:30 "Strive with me as I strive with the Lord…"

9 keys for Striving for agreement in corporate prayer (Romans 15:30):
- Put your whole self into it; try to have the same energy & intensity as the person who leads the effort.
- Let it resonate in your spirit (mean it).
- Get into the mentality and spirit of what God is doing.
- Make sure something is coming out of your mouth: Praise, the name of Jesus, praying in tongues.
- Follow the leader.

- Follow order.
- Don't be so caught up that you can't follow instructions.
- Rid yourself of distractions.
- Learn the language of those you are praying with: (Scriptures, teaching, prophetic utterances, and prayer terminologies).

Note: In Acts 2:1-4, they were all praying, and yet they all heard. This shows how we can't be so caught up in our own prayer mode, and even what we feel God is telling us in prayer, that we end up going in different directions. We could hinder the corporate anointing if we are not alert.

Increasing Intensity in Prayer

Another primary way to increase intensity in prayer is to put the time in. Therefore, prior to examining the remaining three ways to increase intensity in prayer, I would like to first review two reasons why it is necessary to focus time into upgrading your prayer life.

Afterwards, we will review four ways you can apply yourself in actually putting that time in with God in prayer. I know it sounds like a lot, but don't worry, we will review all five principles of increasing intensity in prayer before the conclusion of this chapter.

Putting the Time In

1.) God is a Rewarder of them that diligently seek Him (Hebrews 11:6).

- Rewarder = pay wages

- We are on heaven's payroll. In fact, heaven pays by

the hour.

- Example: Matthew 26:40 – Jesus advised that we pray at least one hour

  - We have to learn how to pray by the hour.
  - Fifteen-minute prayer lives = below minimum wage

2.) Heaven has a Currency System – Revelation 3:18

   a.   In Revelations 3:18, Jesus said, "Buy of me"…

- Buy = heaven's currency system

   b.   In Luke 12:21, 33-34, Jesus mentioned the reality of being "Rich toward God"…

- Rich towards God = we have heavenly accounts

- Prayer is one of the ways we become rich toward God (Luke 12:21, 33). He pays wages when we pray.

- When we become rich towards God, we can receive things that others can't receive because we have paid the price.

Heaven Makes Business Transactions
(Isaiah 55:1)

- Buy without price = make a business transaction with God (Isaiah 55:1).

We can make purchases and exchanges from heaven

without natural currency. This concept of doing business with God is consistent throughout Scripture. In fact, in Luke 19:13, the word "occupy" literally means to do business. It is interesting how scriptures compare our understanding of business transactions with the level of intensity we pray and seek God with (Hebrews 11:6; James 5:16-17).

4 Practical Applications of Putting More Time in with God

The following simply consists of practical insights that I have learned and applied in order to maximize the time I spend with God. They are critical because they help you avoid the pressure of performance and legalism of becoming religious and rigid in your practices of prayer.

1) Speak in tongues as much as possible throughout the day...

- Sometimes we are busy, but every minute counts. My wife and I like to refer to this as "The Wigglesworth Prayer Principle".

- The Wigglesworth Prayer Principle is a method of prayer that my wife and I adopted from Smith Wigglesworth, who is one of God's historic generals in the faith (you should definitely Google and research his history in God). It was once suggested to Wigglesworth that he must have spent hours and hours in prayer in order to see the miracles that he had seen in his ministry over the years. However, Wigglesworth's response was that he often did not spend hours in prayer in one setting, but he rather had of discipline of praying in tongues or meditating on a scripture every 20 minutes.

2) Use prophetic commas while praying...

- Schedule multiple prayer hours throughout the day instead of trying to complete a number of hours in one setting (See Psalms 55:17 & Daniel 6:10).

- Daniel and David were very busy men who worked in government. They didn't always have the time to pray for multiple hours all day. They were both responsible for ordering kingdoms. Therefore, they prayed multiple times a day as seen in Psalms 55:17 and Daniel 6:10.

3) Shut away in prayer until a certain amount of hours are complete.

Sometimes you need hours to build in prayer instead of multiple times throughout the day. You may need to consecrate a day or a couple of days to get away from your busy schedule and put the consistent hours in with God.

4) Shut away until desired result is obtained.

Sometimes you need to take yourself completely off of the clock.

Note: Sometimes we go in and out of prayer using what I call "prophetic commas." At other times, we assign days and weeks of consecration, but there are rare times when we go into prayer and do not come out of prayer at all without an answer, whether it takes hours or days.

Three Additional Ways to Increase Intensity in Prayer

1) Pray fervently in tongues as much as possible.

   1 Corinthians 14: = when you pray in tongues, you edify. Remember to edify means to build up. Therefore, the more you pray in tongues, the more the intensity builds in prayer (See also my book entitled *Experiencing God in the Supernatural Newly Revised*).

2) Wait on the Lord.

   Sometimes fervency is not in the repetition, or aggression that we pray in, but rather the stillness and the surrender. The intensity is more about when all of our passion, focus, and desires are on Jesus. And this most often takes place without words (Isaiah 30:15).

   Refer to chapter three for more notes on what it means to wait on the Lord.

   Note: Sometimes it's good to pray in tongues before we wait on the Lord to focus our minds. Also, we should pray in tongues to get our minds back in synch if they begin to wander.

3) Praise

   • Praise should always be the power source of fervent prayer. The joy of the Lord is our strength.

Daniel's Key:

Daniel 6:10 gives us insight into how Daniel prayed

in ways that wrested down demonic principalities that attempted to control governments. The text says that when he prayed, he gave thanks, which confirms how praise adds intensity to our prayer lives. Through praise, Daniel actually acquired strength in prayer that overthrew the control that the enemy had over governments during those times according to Ezekiel 28. In fact, Daniel was so strong in prayer that even the angels were strengthened as he prayed, which leads to our next chapter where fervent prayer breaks into various realms of the supernatural (Psalm 103:20; Daniel 10:12).

However, let's first review these truths about increasing intensity in prayer. Basically, there are five things you need in order to increase your intensity in prayer as follows: pray in agreement with others; put the time in; pray in tongues as much as possible; wait on the Lord; and keep praise a key part of your prayer life. And that is, of course, in addition to some of the practical application you were given about how to put in more hours with God. It's really that simple.

Chapter 6

Prayer that Breaks into the Supernatural

Lesson Objectives:
— Review how Jesus prayed in ways that opened up supernatural realms.
— Review six signs of breakthrough in prayer and the progressive stages of manifestation.
— Review how to press in and seize atmospheres of breakthrough in prayer.
— Review four things to discern about atmospheric shifts in prayer.
— Review how to overcome feelings of dryness, apathy, or resistance in prayer, and much more.

A Brief Word on Seeking & Knocking

At this point, you understand that there are certain revelations of prayer that go beyond asking and receiving. With that in mind, you should know that seeking and knocking are in fact higher dimensions in prayer than asking and receiving (Matthew 7:7).

In fact, in order to receive in prayer, it is equally important for us to embrace seeking and knocking in prayer to the same extent that we have embraced the principle of asking. They are all valid expressions of prayer, and more in particular, the knocking is not literal, but rather symbolic of the added aggression that we seek God with as we pray.

When we ask, we receive. When we seek, we find, but when we knock, it is opened to us (Matthew 7:7). The question is, however, what is opened?

The answer is that when we knock, there is a supernatural dimension that opens to us in prayer. Jesus prayed into this supernatural dimension, and it is one of the highest dimensions of prayer that we can go into.

Two Examples:

1) Transfiguration:
- Luke 9:29- "as He prayed", He was transfigured right before their eyes:

- Could you imagine praying and all of a sudden:
  - Your skin and physical appearance changes.
  - You have heavenly visitors show up.
  - A cloud surrounds you, and then a voice comes out of the cloud in Dolby surround sound.

2) Walking on Water:
- Matthew 14:23-25

- In vs. 23 He "prayed alone" + vs. 25 He "came out of prayer walking on water"

A Brief Word on Breakthrough in Prayer

It's important we learn how to pray in ways that open up the supernatural dimension. The revelation of who God is and what He wants to do in our lives is in the supernatural dimension. If we can learn to discern the breakthrough in that dimension within the atmosphere of prayer, and properly follow up after the breakthrough, we will see many more manifestations of the supernatural through our prayers.

There are multiple things that take place that are a sign to us that we are breaking through and entering the type of supernatural dimension that Jesus prayed in. If we learn to discern the signs, we can likewise better discern the workings of God in relation to our prayers. The following consists of things that take place in the Spirit when we effectively press into atmospheres of breakthrough.

Six Signs of Breaking Through

1) More Prayer Only Makes You Want to Pray More.

- You transcend flesh (flesh is weak but spirit is willing).

- There is strength to travail.

- The groan of travail becomes the source of new strength (literally & spiritually).

  Note: When you become tired, if you will literally groan, strength will come, but remember to push from your belly and not your own strength. When you really tap in, you will feel as if you can literally pray forever.

2) You Discern Atmospheric Changes & Atmospheric Release (See Also *4 Things to Discern about Atmospheric Shifts in Prayer*).

  a. When there is a shift, you choose how you both respond to it and interact with it.

b. When there is a release, you pray into a particular matter differently.

- Prophetic Gestures: God may have you to do something in the natural that is prophetically symbolic of what He is doing in the Spirit.
- Praise: your praise becomes prophetic of what you believe God has already done. You are no longer asking God to do it, but you are thanking Him that it is already done, although you do not yet see the manifestation.
- Declaration: the things that you originally asked of heaven you begin to command in the earth, because you understand that you have power to speak things into existence.

c. Maintain the atmosphere conducive for manifestation.

- When you sense that the level is dropping you seize the atmosphere and bring the level back up.

3) The Spirit of the Breaker Comes on You.

This includes surges of divine energy, a sense of supernatural momentum, and an experience of Divine force within our prayers. As we pray, there's a fire, and there's a fresh wind.

- Your voice tone changes
- The life of God fills your words
- His voice infuses your voice

Note: We will examine this in more detail from Psalm 29 momentarily as we more examine the spirit of the breaker. For now, the following is a

> *list of additional things that take place under this particular grace in prayer.*

When the Spirit of the Breaker comes, your prayers (a-e):

    a. Break up fallow grounds- Jeremiah 4:3
    b. Remove mountains- Mark 11:23
    c. Prepare a way in the wilderness- Isaiah 40:3
    d. Become weapons of war + fortify walls of protection- 2 Corinthians 10:3
    e. Merge with the prayers of other intercessors- Acts 9:11-12 & Acts16:9-10

4) Your Identity Changes.

- Things that hinder a greater confidence, boldness, and holy aggression break off of your personality.

5) There is a Release of Revelation and You Get Glimpses of the Father's Heart.

- We hear God clearly.
- We commune with the Lord.
- We get instructions, and as we follow them, we see manifestation.
- We encounter the supernatural in various ways.
- Dreams and prophecies come to remembrance, along with understanding, interpretation, and instruction.

6) You Get Lost in God's Presence, and Your Prayer Focuses Adjust to His Desires.

Note: If we understood the power of these stages of breakthrough in prayer we wouldn't get discouraged so easily by what we ignorantly consider as lack of results in prayer.

Four Things to Discern about Atmospheric Shifts in Prayer

DISCERN the source of power (your belly). I couldn't reiterate enough that the way you pray from your belly is by literally using your diaphragm (your stomach area). Scientific studies have proven that this small muscle in your stomach area is the center of all pain and pleasure. In other words, praying from your belly helps you discern what level of passion you are praying with. It keeps you from just going through the religious routines of prayer and stirs in you a hunger for more.

DISCERN the articulation of your tongue. When the atmosphere shifts as you pray, you will often go silent or begin to pray in tongues. And even if you are already praying in tongues, you will either notice that the dialect of your tongue has changed or that the sharpness in the articulation of the tongue has increased.

DISCERN the difference between endurance and strength. Just because you are putting the time in prayer does not necessarily mean that you are breaking through, although you are increasing in intensity. You have to be mature enough to realize the difference between you being able to endure long periods in prayer and when the strength of God actually comes into your prayer time.

DISCERN the rising intensity levels when there is an atmospheric shift and actively participate. If not you will only be going through the motions in prayer.

NOTE: Imagine prayer as a vehicle that you are driving with the intent of arriving at an intended destination. The more you experience breakthrough, the more you will discern when to accelerate the gas in prayer in order to avoid praying in "cruise control." The reality is that without discernment, you may end up praying under the "speed limit" and not even know it. In fact, when you cultivate discernment in prayer, you will know when you need to accelerate and you will also know when to put the brakes on to avoid praying in your own strength and flesh.

Although utilizing your strength is necessary when pressing in, it is yet useless in accomplishing real and lasting victories in prayer. Breakthrough is not something we can conjure in prayer; however, we must cooperate with it.

There is a sensitivity involved in discerning and learning how to press in enough to keep with God's movements in prayer, and yet know when to back up enough and not to get ahead. However, those who fail to develop this discernment will often back up when they should be pressing in or press in when they should be backing up.

This is why one of the most important things to discern in corporate prayer is WHO TO FOLLOW. You cannot afford to adopt the dead religious routines in prayer that you may often observe in the lives of those whose only objective of praying in a public setting is to impress people. And those who lead in corporate settings of prayer should be those who have developed the necessary discernment in order to do so.

Cooperate prayer is the best training ground for those who desire to break into supernatural dimensions of prayer. However, those who deceive themselves into thinking that they are following the Spirit's leading more than they are wiling to follow the experienced leading of someone who is proven in God will miss the impartation.

Pressing In

Pressing into God in Prayer Really Consist of two Things...

1) Wait until He comes.
2) Stay until He is finished.

We Must be Willing to Press In ...

The key is desire. You simply cannot allow your flesh to rule your prayer life. Flesh never wants to pray—no matter how spiritual you get or think you are. It will help you to remember that every time we pray, it is only because God gave us the desire to (Psalm 37:4).

More on the Spirit of the Breaker

When we break through in prayer:

- Remember, there is a new source of boldness and confidence in our tone of voice.
- Our words become more like declarations and they legislate Divine law.
- Remember, His voice infuses our voices (Psalm 29) + our tongues change (tongues of angels).
- Remember, the energy and life of God fills our words when we press past feelings and even our own intensity and volume.

Three Verses in Psalm 29:1-9 Brings More Clarity on How God's Voice Infuses Ours

1.) Vs.5 the voice breaks the cedar

- Cedar = the hardest resisting wood
- Breaking a cedar would be the closest equivalent to penetrating brass ceilings or cracking a steel wall.

2.) Vs.8 the voice shakes the wilderness

- Remember, the voice carries with it the power to turn a miserable place into a paradise (Isaiah 51:3) & Remember, it prepares the way in wilderness (Isaiah 40:3).

3.) Vs.7 the voice divides flames

- Dividing flames requires bending elements + adjusting laws of nature. It represents how all things become possible to those that believe as they pray.

A Brief Word on Praying in Tongues From Your Belly

Praying in tongues is one of the greatest ways to break through in prayer. And more so when we pray from our bellies in tongues, there is both an awareness of where our prayer power source originates, and there is an added measure of fervency (John 7:37). What I mean by this is that the push literally comes from your diaphragm (stomach area).

When we pray in tongues with a force from our belly, it is almost as if we register our voices in the heavens. You can sense the difference in your tone and in the articulation of your tongues. It's beyond words, because the scriptures say that it is our spirit that is doing the praying (1 Corinthians 14:14). This means that the prayer is originating from our innermost being, which again means that the source of the articulation is not from our diction, but from our belly.

Think of it as if not praying from your belly is equivalent to talking to someone in a language that they do not understand. Therefore, if we are going to be effective praying in tongues from our belly, the key is that we can't think more than we pray. When praying in this realm, if you're thinking, your thoughts should be consumed with either making sure you are praying from your belly or how awesome God is and how badly you want more of His presence and power to be evident in your life.

If you do not understand what I'm communicating, don't worry, you will soon enough. One day, if you press in long enough, you will experience this reality and you will be able to refer back to this writing with greater clarity. I recommend you read my first book *Experiencing God in the Supernatural Newly Revised* for more powerful truths concerning praying in tongues.

Review Results of Spirit-Led Prayer in Romans 8:26-34:

- Vs.26 – The Holy Spirit picks up our inability to pray and upgrades our prayer lives.
- Vs.28 – All things work together.
- Vs. 28 – and we know all things work = we get heaven's perspective concerning where we are
- Vs. 29 – conformed to His image = our identity is changed (Sonship)
- Vs. 30 – There is a constant awareness and assurance of our salvation.
- Vs. 31 – No enemies can stand against us.
- Vs. 32 – freely gives us all things = we prophetically become aware of what is released in prayer.
- Vs. 33-39 – We are assured of our salvation and victory on Christ.

The Wow Factor

The wow factor is based on vs.28 from the previous list that lets us know that all things work together for our good. It is when we experience sudden surprises in God due to our consistency to seek God and our constant dependence on His best interest for us at heart. I know it is a familiar verse, but we rarely teach it in the context that it was written in, which was the context of prayer.

When we find ourselves in Romans 8:28 kind of prayer, it is a place in which we can't judge what God is doing in the atmosphere based on how we feel. Neither can we judge it by what we see or do not see manifesting. But if we keep pressing in prayer, we will find that God is actually exceeding our expectations.

As we develop a track record of praying into a supernatural realm, we realize that some of the things that we considered as merely an "unanswered prayer" were rather God working all things in our favor. We discover that we were either aiming too low in our requests, or we were not ready for many of the things that we believed for.

This is one reason why God exceeds in abundance above all we can ask or think. And most importantly, we develop maturity in the process as we learn to discern and pray God's will for our lives more accurately.

Six Basics in Developing Maturity in Prayer:

- Develop patience and obedience.
- Develop an accuracy concerning where we are in our spiritual walk.
- Be faithful and aware of where we are in the process of moving forward from where we are.
- Keep pressing in for more: you can't lose hunger and become stagnant.
- If you find yourself in a place of discouragement, don't remain there.
- Avoid distractions.
- Develop an understanding that in all labor there is profit, and that whatever you sow, you will reap because of the fact that God will not be mocked

(Proverbs 14:23; Galatians 6:7)
- DEVELOP LOVE FOR GOD'S PRESENCE and His people ABOVE ALL ELSE.

A Brief Word on the History of Breaking into Supernatural Realms of Prayer

There is a pinnacle in prayer that extends beyond breakthrough atmospheres. If we will press past flesh, emotions, and even the surge of energy; there is a glory that far exceeds the excitement of spiritual momentum that becomes even more unprecedented.

In this place, God can trust us with more because we've developed the kind of maturity in prayer that understands prayer as being much more than a means for us to convince God to grant us our requests. We understand that prayer is a place where we encounter God and know the realities of His kingdom.

When we mature in prayer, we prize the presence of God over anything He could ever give us. In fact, most times we find ourselves praying not to receive anything, but to rather get lost in the awe of His majesty.

We pray fervently because we have come to know a rest that we can labor to enter into (Hebrews 4:11). And in that rest, we understand that everything we will ever need is already done (Hebrews 4:3-11). And most importantly, we get so raptured in the ecstasy of who God is that the things He has to offer pale in comparison to our love for His presence.

When God finds a group of people that understand this place in prayer, there is often a supernatural element evident in their times of prayer. He often willingly displays His wonders to them because they have become so in love with Him that they will never fanaticize over His signs.

Trust me, your prayer will take on a different dynamic when you have the realization that God is there as opposed to a mentality of hoping to get His attention. The following are only a few examples throughout history of those who broke into this kind of supernatural dimension as they approached God in prayer.

After reviewing the following, you should do a little homework and discover more throughout scripture. Look at the following scriptures in another light, and I guarantee you will never take prayer lightly again or approach your time in prayer as a religious duty that you dread to fulfill. You will begin to break into a supernatural dimension in prayer, and you will never be the same.

Those Who Broke Into The Supernatural in Prayer

- After Moses had prayed and fasted eighty days, his face began to glow (Exodus 43:29).

- When Daniel prayed, an angel came to him (Daniel 9:21).

- When Jesus prayed, He was transfigured (Luke 9:29).

- After Jesus prayed, He walked on water (Matthew 14:23-25).

- After the early church prayed, the grounds shook (Acts 4:31).

- When Peter prayed, he went into a trance (Acts 10:9-10).

- When John prayed, Jesus appeared to him, and he was caught up into the throne room of God. (Revelations 1:10-20; Revelations 4).

Note: As we conclude this chapter, again, I recommend you read my first book *Experiencing God in the Supernatural Newly Revised* and meditate on the various levels of revelation that you will learn in it rather from the perspective of prayer.

Chapter 7

Persistence in Prayer

Lesson Objectives:
- Review why persistence in prayer is necessary.
- Review eight hindrances to answered prayer.
- Review six protocols of preparation for engaging warfare prayer and much more.

Persistence is Key

There is great reason that I would like to deal with persistence in prayer in conclusion to phase one of this book. And the reality is that everything you have learned so far will still require patience, consistency, and process in order for you see the results that you truly desire to see in prayer (and this is not even the half of what you will experience by the time you finish the book).

This is key because there are many who are easily discouraged due to the lack of intended results as they pray. However, we cannot afford to grow weary, because we will reap if we don't faint (Galatians 6:9).

Truth is, after we have done all we know to do in prayer, there are reasons that prayers are not answered immediately at times. Therefore, I want to take the time to examine some of the reasons so that you are able to persevere through the delay that may occur.

Three Reasons that Prayers are not Answered

As you study the following three reasons that prayers are not answered, you will actually learn over eight hindrances to answered prayers, and how to overcome them.

1.) Sometimes we just have to wait:

Why do we have to wait? Take a look at points **a**, **b**, and **c** for three reasons that we wait.

a.) Character development:

- At times God is working "in us" rather than "for us."

- Affliction will often be included in order to accomplish this.

- (Psalm 119:71) Affliction = Learning, instruction, understanding, revelation, wisdom

Romans 5 explains this process in more detail as follows:

- Romans 5:3-5 – Glory also in tribulations...

- Romans 5:3-5 is teaching us what to do when we are presented with the opposite of what the word of God promises us; we YET glory in it.

- Romans 5:3-5 also details to us the process of character development as follows:

Dissecting Romans 5:3-4, verse by verse, in order to Understand God's Process of Character Development

- Vs. 3 – Tribulations produce patience, which is defined as "persevering endurance and fortitude."

- Vs. 4 – Patience produces experience, which is defined as "maturity of character and tried integrity." (Note: God will allow us to be in situations where we must endure so that He can develop character.)

- Vs.4 – Experience produces hope, which is defined as "habit of joy, confidence, and constant rejoicing." (Note: In other words, we are developing a character that is evident in our attitude and lifestyle.)

The Second Reason We Wait Is:

b.) Sowing and Reaping = Praying is sowing (Galatians 6:28; Hosea 10:12)

- Matthew 13:24-30 – Sometimes we get discouraged because the wheat and tares grow together during harvest time. We feel as if we are doing right, yet bad things take place. We forget all the times that we have sown in the flesh.

So what do we do?

- Matthew 13:30 – Take all of the harvest (good & bad) and separate it later; focus on the good so that when the next season of harvest comes, the good seed outweighs the bad.

The Third and Last Reason We Wait Is:

c.) Time & season: Everything God does and expects us to do is connected to time and season.

- We have to pray in alignment with time and season, so that we won't be expecting God to prioritize something that is not His intended purpose for that season.

Note: Timing shouldn't be used as a "cop-out" for

unanswered prayer. Also, there are ways that we can get God to move early before season and out of season on our behalf: John 2:1-11, Hebrews 6:5...

...YET, if we find ourselves in a season of waiting, we should not get discouraged; we should simply persist in prayer.

2.) The second reason that prayers are not answered is simply because the request is denied:

At times, there are reasons that our prayers will not be answered, with the exception of prayers of repentance or prayers of rescue out of immediate danger. See the following for a list of reasons that certain prayer requests are denied:

a) Lack of obedience – Hebrews 10:36, 6:12. (Promises are conditional)

b) Sin – Psalm 66:18

c) Praying amiss – (wrong thing at wrong time). James 4:1-4 = Fleshly desires, trials, ignorance.

d) Sloth & lack of fervency – James 5:16-18 (you need strength to birth- Isaiah 37:3)

e) Wrong relationships – 1 Peter 3:7 & Matthew 5:23-24 (husbands, wives, children, friends, and etc.)

f) God has "something better." – Hebrews 11:39-40

"When God has Something Better"

James 1:2-5 – "If any man lacks wisdom, let him ASK" =

Scripture teaches that the first thing to pray for in a trial is wisdom, and while asking for wisdom, we are instructed to maintain our praise.

Why ask for wisdom?

- (James 1:3-4) If the trial comes to teach patience, it should be evidence to us, at that point, that anything else we ask for we will not receive it when we want it anyway, so we might as well ask for wisdom.

- Nine times out of ten, answers to prayer seem to be put on hold in the midst of a trial. This means that everything we had on the top of our prayer list, God pushes to the bottom. Wisdom, praise, and patience become His priority according to James 1:2-5.

- Good news is that God works patience "in us" so that ultimately patience will work "for us."

- James 1:4 – The Perfect work of patience is that we lack (want) NOTHING.

- When patience finishes working, there will be NO LACK.

- Patience = Don't get discouraged when it looks like prayers are not working.

  When it seems as if prayers are not being answered, it only means that God is going to give us more than what we originally asked for, and in the end, there will be NO LACK in our lives (James 1:4).

3.) The last reason that prayers are not answered is because at times there is warfare:

- We must learn to utilize prayer in overcoming demonic hindrances (Daniel 10:12-13).

- In cases where prayers are not answered due to demonic interference, we must be properly prepared for the battle, and there are six protocols that will help us in the process.

Six Protocols of Preparation for Engaging Warfare Prayer

1.) Know that God is fighting your battles (Deut. 1:30).

2.) Never take it lightly + live sober (1 Peter 5:8-9).

3.) Make sure you're covered – There are some basic healthy Christian disciplines that should be implemented in our lives prior to any attempt of engaging spiritual battle such as prayer, fasting, tithing, giving, submission to authority, witnessing, etc. We should be sure that we are not overlooking the foundational things as we progress in God. We should be mindful that we are living lifestyles of repentance, humility, and Godly character overall as well. When we willingly refuse to obey what the scriptures teach concerning the basics of foundational Christian living, there are areas that can remain uncovered and unprotected from demonic retaliation in spiritual warfare.

How?

○ 2 Corinthians 10:6 teaches that it is only when our obedience is fulfilled that we can avenge all disobedience.

- o Therefore, we must be sure we are not giving the enemy an open door through disobedience.

Examples:
- Cain: Genesis 4:7 = sin at the door.
- Peter: Matthew 16:23 = Jesus said, "get behind me, satan" when rebuking Peter. And although Peter was powerful in God, the enemy was able to find an open door in his heart.

What's the Point?

- John 14:30 – Jesus said that the devil had no part in Him + Ephesians 4:27 instructs us to give no place to the devil.

- We want to do a regular checkup to know how healthy we are in our Christian lifestyle, because the enemy will attempt to gain ground in areas of our lives that are not properly fortified.

The Six Protocols Continued...

4.) Pray in the Spirit (Jude 20).

5.) Dress for battle

Put on:
- The Blood
- The Lord Jesus Christ (Romans 13:14; Galatians 5:19-20)
- The Whole Armor (Ephesians 6:13-17; Romans 13:12; 2 Corinthians 6:7)

6.) Resist the devil – There are some battles we can avoid if we just stand in authority (James 4:7).

James 4:7
- Resist = Stand steadfast = Understand your authority (Psalm 149)

 As We:
   - Worship
   - War with the Prophecy
   - & Make Declarations...

 We Acknowledge the legal grounds of our victory through Christ according to Ephesians 3:10.

Ready for Basic Training in Battle

Congratulations, you have officially completed phase one of *Boot Camp Prayer* manual. Now you are ready to be trained in the art of spiritual warfare prayer. However, you will need to be sure that you use this book as a reference guide from here on out.

Chapter 8

Learning the Art of War

Chapter Objective:
Review four prayer focuses important in engaging spiritual battle

Phase Two

Welcome to phase two of *Boot Camp Prayer*. If you have made it this far, it is because you are serious about becoming skilled in prayer, and you are progressing because of the knowledge that you are beginning to apply.

However, your next level of effectiveness in prayer will include you actually being engaged in the spiritual battle that is waged in the spirit realm. This phase of your training is specifically devoted into making you into an effective spiritual warrior, and teaching you how to deploy your divine arsenal and weaponry. Now, let's get straight to the point.

The majority of our modern-day warfare prayer practices are not as effective as we think they are. In fact, many individuals are habitually religious in their practices of what they assume warfare prayer to be. However, if we are going to really be effective in the battle, we have to eventually consider the fact that there should be more notable victories being experienced in the body of Christ as a whole if there is truly as much spiritual warfare going on as we have portrayed.

Many times when individuals think of warfare

prayer, they think of binding the devil and rebuking demons. Many end up running into battle either unprepared, not knowing how to engage in battle, or not knowing what they are getting into. But in reality, warfare prayer is just what it says it is. It is warfare prayer. Let me explain.

The word *war* in scripture is derived from a Greek word from which we have the word *strategy*. The revelation is that warfare prayer is strategic prayer. It is praying in a strategic way that ensures our victory. This means that if we are not praying strategically, we are not properly engaged in the war.

Therefore, there are four primary focuses that we should strategically pray into continually in spiritual battle that I would like to show you over the remaining chapters. Each focus consists of multiple facets, and there are also many battle tactics needed in order to effectively engage the war around each focus. The focuses are as follows:

1) Ask the Lord to reveal who your enemy is.
2) Ask the Lord to enforce the victory already granted to you.
3) Ask for a battle plan, and that is only if the Lord specifically directs you to further engage the battle, which I will explain in detail later.
4) Lastly, you want to actually engage the battle in prayer.

Now, before you underestimate the previous list, I want to warn you that what you are about to read is going to be power-packed with a plethora of invaluable secrets in prayer. You will embrace many battle tactics and maneuvers in prayer, such as how to counterattack the enemy, how to properly bind and loose, how to deploy the spiritual weapons in your divine arsenal, and that's not even the half of it. You want to be sure your heart and mind are open as we now begin to examine each facet of our prayer focuses one by one.

Chapter 9

The Demonic Hierarchy

Chapter Objectives:
- Understand the difference between demons and demonic structures.
- Understand why it is important to expose demonic ranks, and how it helps in our approach to the battle and perspective of spiritual warfare.
- Understand various demonic ranks, what they represent, and much more.

Prayer focus #1 in the Art of War

Jesus taught on the importance of counting up the cost prior to engaging war. This partially represents how you must have an assessment of your enemy and his tactics so that you are not ignorant of his devices. The objective is that you want to know your enemy's strategies, weaponry, manpower, etc. You then want to consider the facts, and determine whether or not the fight is worth your attention.

Therefore, the first prayer focus in the art of war is to know your enemy, in which we must expose multiple demonic ranks in order to do so. However, I write this under the assumption that you already understand the importance of the first, knowing our God and His promises concerning our lives. I am assuming that the Lord has already revealed who He is to you and what His promises are to you in your situation before you attempt to engage a spiritual battle. If not, you definitely want to make that a prerequisite because therein lies your victory.

Jonathan Ferguson

Now I must warn you that from this point on, I will write much on exposing key demonic workings. However, you will find that beyond this first prayer focus, the majority of my writing will not be focused on the demonic, but more so on our victory over the demonic. I want you to be sure that this is not a book on demonology, but rather our authority in Jesus over the forces of darkness through prayer.

Demonic Ranks of Rule

In Ephesians 6:18, Paul is teaching prayer in the context of spiritual warfare. He is teaching that if we are going to pray effectively, we have to understand that we are praying in a hostile environment. We have to understand that we are in a battle. And not only that, but we must also understand the nature of the battle if we are going to war effectively.

This is why in Ephesians 6:12, the scripture begins to expose the various ranks of demonic powers. In doing so, we begin to understand the operations of our enemy so that we can strategically counter them.

Expanded Demonology

In order to understand the concept of demonic ranks, we must understand the difference between demons and demonic structures. In reality, it is one thing to understand demons, but understanding the governmental structure of the demonic world requires us to expand our understanding of demonology. Truth is, the understanding of demonic ranks reaches far beyond the typical theology of demonic possession and oppression.

Simply put, a demonic structure is a hierarchy, a chain of command, or a coalition of demonic powers. In fact, principalities and powers are the most mentioned biblically of this hierarchy. They work in the second heavens so that answers to prayers and the manifestation of God's promises are prohibited, frustrated, or delayed. They seek to ultimately overthrow the plans of God and advance the kingdom of darkness in the earth.

Exposing Demonic Ranks

In Ephesians 6:12, there is a governmental/military-structured chain of authority. There are four ranks of demonic powers that are mentioned from highest rank down to the lowest ranking. These demonic ranks operate in high places or what is better known as the spirit realm.

This is key because God wants us to understand that the real battle is in the spirit realm. This is why the scriptures say that we do not wrestle against flesh and blood, and that the weapons of our warfare are not carnal. In other words, if we are going to overcome demonic opposition, we have to do so from another dimension beyond the natural, because we are not in a natural battle.

You are reading this book because you understand that there is a war being waged. However, such an acknowledgement is not enough to equip you to be victorious in battle. Can I prophesy to you? If you are going to become an effective warrior, you are going to have to realize that many of the ways in which many attempt spiritual warfare actually result in their demise.

The truth is that if we really understood the demonic hierarchy that we are up against, we would likewise understand that the majority of the church's approach to spiritual warfare is wrong. In fact, many have experienced serious war causalities due to misinformed attempts of engaging the spiritual battle. This must change.

However, I want to reiterate that we cannot war effectively if we do not understand the nature of the battle. And the only way to truly understand the nature of the battle is to understand the demonic ranks and how they operate. Therefore, I want to now begin detailing the demonic hierarchy one by one and give insight concerning their operations.

The Demonic Hierarchy

1) Principalities: archomai = 1st in rank and order

The word principality is derived from the Greek word *archomai*. In fact, the root word for *archomai* is *arch*, from which the word prince is derived, and it means to be first in rank.

Therefore, according to the previous information, the next thing we should understand is that a principality is not merely a demon. A principality is rather a demonic structure that requires both a prince and its principal of rule in order to exist.

It consists of a ruling spirit, its fortress, and its succession of ranks. It is both the strongman and the stronghold that the strongman rules from.

The truth is that a principality cannot operate apart from a demonic fortress, which is referenced in 2 Corinthians 10:3 as a stronghold. In fact, the word stronghold is by definition a fortress. Therefore, the mentioning of strongholds in scripture is part of a bigger picture.

Many of you reading have most likely never heard principalities explained in reference to strongmen, let alone a stronghold mentioned in reference to a demonic headquarters. However, it helps to understand that a strongman is mentioned in more than one light in scripture. One is in reference to spirits that seek to possess individuals, and another is in reference to ruling spirits that seek to govern territories.

It's also important to consider that in order to understand principalities, we should understand that 2 Corinthians 10 gives us insight into HOW strongholds exist, but Ephesians 2 and Ephesians 6 rather give insight into WHY they exist. Simply put, strongholds serve as demonic headquarters for ruling spirits. Principalities cannot establish themselves in a region without establishing a stronghold.

Once a stronghold is established, a prince demon then has a place from which they can govern their principalities as a type of demonic headquarters, and they are given authority to act in the name of the devil. Principalities can range in size; their rule can extend over nations, regions, cities, or even small groups (Proverbs 28:2). There is a well-organized chain of command in which the next in authority among the demonic ranks, after that of a prince, is what the scripture refers to as powers.

2) Powers: Exousia = delegated authorities

Demonic powers are, by definition, delegated authorities within the demonic hierarchy. More specifically, wherever there is a principality, the first in authority would be a prince, and the next in line would be a power.

In fact, prince demons and demonic powers go hand in hand. They operate like Presidents and Vice Presidents, captain and co-captain.

Have you noticed that there is almost never a time in scripture in which principalities and powers are not mentioned simultaneously? The mentioning of them together is often a short way of acknowledging that there is a chain of command among both the angelic world and the demonic world.

Powers are also in reference to the demonic influences upon the leaders in high positions, luring them into lawlessness or luring them to cross over into demonic manifestations of the supernatural via occult practices and psychic mediums. Many examples of this activity can be found in the books of Exodus and Daniel. Scripture goes into great detail concerning the confrontation of Moses and Daniel against the various types of satanic priests that operated in the Egyptian, Babylonian, and Persian cultures servicing their kings.

Demonic powers target people in authority because the more individuals yield their influence over to a principality, the more the principality can expand its rule. And most of the time, these evil spirits appeal to people in authority no different than how the devil appealed to Jesus. They offer more authority in exchange for immorality and sin, and the individual takes it not knowing that in actuality, they are giving more authority away than they are receiving.

Even today there are governmental and business leaders that seek out teams of occult leaders who supply the spiritual forces necessary to promote their agendas. This means that when dealing with a strongman, we have to understand that there will often be an individual who has come into covenant with and acts in representation for the demonic power that we are confronting. Therefore, when strongholds are to be pulled down, we should realize that at times it would call for individuals to lose political office, economic status, or even cultural influence.

I am not in any way claiming to understand everything there is to understand about this chain of command. All I know is what the Lord wants to be revealed in the pages of this book. And even beyond what you are learning so far, there is more that you will learn concerning how principalities and powers operate beyond the activities of the occult. However, for now, let's continue to briefly understand the remaining demonic ranks.

3) Rulers: kosmokrator/skotos = officers

Rulers by definition are high-ranking demonic officers. I like to think of them as either lieutenants or special ops forces. They are employed for special tasks or either assigned to patrol, surveillance, and manage territories in which there are demonic headquarters set up.

4) Hosts:

This particular ranking consists of only the authority that a soldier, police officer, or even a security guard would have. Their responsibility is in executing at ground level the orders of the demonic delegates they serve. Their nature consists of anything warped, perverted, depraved, debased, dysfunctional, and corrupt (host of wickedness).

These are the demons within the demonic ranks that seek to inhabit and possess human bodies, or at the very least oppress an individual. And remember, they are not called a host for no reason. A list of these various types of demons would prove to be beyond extensive. However, there are more angels that are for us than all of the demons of hell against us.

The key is not to try and learn every demon by name because the classifications are exhaustive. There are some that are recognized by specific names, while others by a general personification of evil. For example, at times Jesus would cast demons out by name, and at other times He would merely address them as unclean spirits (Mark 5:9; Luke 6:18; 8:29).

Lastly, when dealing with evil spirits that seek to inhabit bodies, we should understand and remember that a strongman is not in reference to a ruling spirit, but a specific demon that hosts the expression of multiple evil personalities or vices. Furthermore, there are only ten to twelve actual names of specific demons mentioned in the bible. They are believed to be the strongmen by which every other evil spirit that seeks possession exists and operate.

Recommended reading for more study on this level of demonic activity include: *Strongman: What's his name & What's his Game*. I would also HIGHLY recommend Benny Hinn's teaching on demons and demonology.

My job in this book is not to go into great details concerning this level of demonic activity. I am rather to give you a general overview of the demonic hierarchy at large in an attempt to cause an adjustment in your perspective concerning the battle at hand. Our next agenda is to understand how they operate so that we can in turn understand the level of strategy required to oppose them.

Chapter 10

Targets & Core Operations of Demonic Ranks

Chapter Objectives:
- Learn three main targets of principalities and powers.
- Understand eight cultural agendas of principalities and powers, and how they establish strongholds in these areas.
- Learn the importance of accurately discerning spiritual conflicts, how it affects the way we war, and much more.

Now that we somewhat understand the ranks of our demonic foes, we should understand their targets and operations, and in doing so, we will understand the nature of the battle. Demonic ranks have specific targets—period. In fact, the targets are mostly corporate and not personal in nature.

There are many who feel as if the devil is coming against them, when in reality he is not. Only seven individuals in scripture had direct confrontation with the devil himself. They were: Eve, Job, Moses, David, Jesus, Peter, and Paul. The devil is not ever-present, neither is he all-powerful. Therefore, even he has to choose his battles.

The revelation is that many times we feel the heat of the battle and retaliate in an attempt of spiritual warfare, not knowing that in reality we are not overcoming any demonic forces because we are not even in the battle. You will understand this more as we further expose demonic targets and I explain the importance of discerning the nature of the struggle. But for now, lets cover the three main targets of demonic ranks.

#1 Territories

In Daniel 10, an angel makes reference to a prince of Persia who was blocking Daniel's prayers. Therein the angel was giving Daniel revelation concerning the spiritual activity that was taking place in and above Persia. There was a Prince demon that had associated itself with Persian territory. It had also established a stronghold in its atmosphere and it was only through prayer that Daniel was able to make war with its agenda and penetrate its demonic resistance.

This account of Daniel provides scriptural support to why many refer to principalities and powers as territorial spirits. It is in Daniel 10 that we clearly see these demonic powers working in the spiritual realm to influence natural territories. We have to have awareness that for every city or nation represented, there is a spiritual realm that is also represented. Furthermore, the governing spiritual entity in that spiritual territory or realm has the ability to influence the activities within that particular corresponding natural territory. This is why we must take authority in the Spirit so that the enemy is not claiming our grounds.

In Ezekiel 9, there are references to angels that have charge over particular cities. David also understood this when he made a prophetic declaration to principalities and powers that the King of Glory was coming in whether they wanted to open access to Him or not in Psalm 24.

The man with the legion of demons is another great example of how territories are often under the influence of either demonic or angelic authorities. The scripture states that because of the demonic activity in one man, the whole country was in fear—even after the fact that the man was delivered. Not to mention that when Jesus did cast the evil spirits out of the man, they begged Jesus not to make them leave the region. I think that anyone who has noticed the facts of that particular story would be convinced that the evil spirits that were manifesting at the tombs were after the territory and not just the man possessed with the legions.

The truth is, there are certain areas and lands that are more inclined to certain evils based on the principalities and powers established therein. We should be aware of this, as we are in an attempt to claim ground for the Kingdom of God. This means that some warfare could actually be attributed to certain geographical locations. However, if we learn to properly deal with the powers of the air, we will find that as a result, we are able to advance more and claim more territory for the kingdom of God.

#2 Generations

In Daniel 10, another thing that we notice in Daniel's conflict is that after the angel gives Daniel insight into the spiritual battle being waged over Persia, he then mentions how he was next to contend with the prince of Greece. This is significant because historically, Persia was the leading power at that time, and Greece was next in line. The fact is that after Daniel begins to gain the upper hand in the spiritual battle waging over Persia, the enemy immediately began to attack generationally in targeting the next super power, which was Greece.

Daniel was literally in one generation waging battle over powers attempting to influence the next generation and era of governmental power. The battle of the ages has

95

always been over the seed. Not only is the enemy strategically warring against generations to come, but also there are demonic forces of the generations past that frequently resurface in an attempt to resist the will of God in the earth. They are what many others and I refer to as ancient demons. Our conflict with such evil spirits today is no different than one of the seven churches in the book of Revelation's conflict with the spirit of Jezebel as it resurfaced nearly 1000 years after Elijah having first dealt with her. Selah

#3 Culture and World Systems

In John 12, Jesus makes mention of the prince of this world. This is significant because in the New Testament, the word *world* is translated from two Greek words. One word is *aeon* and it deals with culture, times, and trends.

The other word is *kosmos*, and is defined as systems or an ordered arrangement. For example, economics, government, and education are all referred to as systems. They are key concerning the overall makeup of our world's civilization.

They are an "ordered arrangement" of institutions that shape our societies and drive the progress of humanity. In fact, the root word for kosmos is komidzo, which means to provide for. In other words, these systems are designed to provide the optimum earth experience and derive from key values of life that God instituted in Eden.

These systems can also be referred to as social stratas, mountains, kingdoms, higher powers, institutions, pillars of societies, and molders of culture. Some say there are seven; others say there are ten or twelve. However, the exact phraseology and numbering of such is not as important as understanding the concept.

The concept is that this is how our world functions. This is life as we know it and as God has ordered it. Let me make this plain. In Eden, God gave us life and placed us in a sphere where there was family, government, prosperity, recreation, education, and every other provision we needed in order to advance and have the optimum earth experience.

We should understand that it is not ok for us to be professional at doing church, but have no significant involvement in the systems that drive the progress of human life as we know it. We should also understand that the enemy is not as concerned with attacking our lives as much as he is in controlling these systems.

The enemy knows that if he can control these systems he can, through them, dramatically alter life and culture. Therefore, in warfare prayer, we have to understand that it means nothing if we are spending our time rebuking devils, but not equipping individuals to dominate the stages and platforms of the various world systems they are called to serve the kingdom of God on.

Eight Major Cultural Agendas of Demonic Principalities

1) Determine the prevailing opinion (what's trending).
2) Determine how policies are formed.
3) Determine quality of family & education= how families are raised/instructed (Note: the moral decline that led to the flood began with the first man that had two wives).
4) Determine where we invest money + they determine what resources that people gather to support which agendas.
5) Determine what we see as moral + spectrum between entertainment and perversion.

6) Determine leadership support and votes.
7) Determine the way we value faith.
8) Determine career objectives.

By targeting culture and world systems, principalities and powers seek to control the prevailing opinion, economy, thought, attitude, and morality of the people. Particularly in our generation, they utilize mass communication and media to propagate demonic ideas, agendas, beliefs, philosophies, etc. Once media exposure occurs, these demonic ideas are then articulated in:

- Politics
- Music arts & entertainment
- News media/gossip
- Movies, etc.

Other key strategies & targets of principalities and powers to be mindful of include:

Daniel 7:25

- They seek to wear us out: frustrations, hindrances, limitations, and stress.

- They seek to change times: cycles, patterns, delay of prophecy, iniquity, history, and trends.

- They seek to change laws: covenants, agreements, contracts, legislation/bills, ordinances, lawsuits, and new world order.

How Do Principalities and Powers Operate?

In order to understand the operation of these demonic ranks that are mentioned in Ephesians 6:12, we must merge the truths in Ephesians 2:1-2 and 2 Corinthians 10:3. It is only as we merge all three scriptural texts that we understand the relationship of demonic princes, powers, atmospheres, strongholds, culture, and world systems. Let's first cover the basics.

We have to remember that it is important to understand the truths recorded in both Ephesians 2:1-2 and 2 Corinthians 10:3 because a principality is not merely a demon, but rather it is a demonic structure. It is evident that a demonic prince alone cannot make up a principality that Ephesians 6:12 makes mention of. I reiterate, that in order to make up a principality, a demonic prince would need a fortress or garrison from which to head its operations, and also it would need to delegate a chain of command.

Remember, the reality of the demonic prince is found in Ephesians 2:1-2. However, the reality of the demonic fortress from which it operates is found in 2 Corinthians 10:3. Therefore, it is only as we merge the two that we not only understand what a principality is, but also how it operates.

Prince + pality = Ephesians 2:2 + 2 Corinthians 10:3 = principalities and powers

If we study the scriptures and do the math. we learn that principalities and powers are working in the atmosphere (air) to create strongholds. Once the stronghold is established in an atmosphere as the predominate mentality of the people, demonic cultures can then begin to infiltrate and dominate world systems. There are a lot of truths in Ephesians 2 alone that when dissected, will help us understand this truth.

Briefly Dissecting Ephesians 2

As we have previously mentioned, Ephesians 2 mentions not only a prince, but also the powers of the air, of which the air specifically has to do with atmosphere. Therefore, a spiritual atmosphere is simply power that is accessible in the air. It is a felt influence in the earth of the activity that takes place in a spiritual realm.

Another significant thing that Ephesians 2 mentions is "the courses of this world." It teaches that there are courses that are established in accordance to the powers of the air. If we examine the phrase "courses of the world," in Ephesians 2 from the Greek text, we find both the words *kosmos* and *aeon*.

Lastly, we would only need to remember the definitions of the words kosmos and aeon, and compare the truths of Ephesians 2:1-2, Ephesians 6:12, and 2 Corinthians 10:3 in order to expose the workings of the demonic ranks. In a nutshell, the reality that we discover is how demonic powers work in the atmosphere in order to create the culture, the timing, and the trends of this world's systems.

According to Ephesians 2, in order to create culture, they must set courses. And in order to set courses, they must control the air. And this is where Ephesians 2 merges with 2 Corinthians 10, because in order to control the air, they must establish strongholds. And in order to establish strongholds, they must first gain access into our minds.

You can always tell what spirit is dominating the air by the mentality of the people. Whatever presence dominates the atmosphere will influence our thought process the most. Ephesians 2 is simply explaining to us why principalities and powers work in the atmosphere to create strongholds. They have to establish strongholds in order to influence culture and demonically alter world systems.

How do Principalities and Powers Establish Strongholds?

I want to reiterate how, according to 2 Corinthians 10, in order to establish a stronghold, the enemy has to first get into our psyches. Therefore, we must understand that these are sophisticated demons that are waging battle against our minds. They are more so subtle than they are lethal, initially.

The enemy knows that if he is going to get into our psyches, then he has to seduce our souls. This is our mind, will, and emotions (I feel, I think, I want). In fact, the battle is not merely over our minds, but also the spirit of our minds, which includes our consciousness, morality, moods, thoughts, attitudes, intentions, etc. In other words, the enemy is after the heart. Therefore, he has to go through the same process the word of God has to go through in order to enter in our hearts.

He has to make sure his agenda is in our mouth, before our eyes, and in our ears because they are gateways into our hearts. If he is going to create a stronghold, then he has to make sure we are always hearing what he is saying, saying what he is saying, and seeing it like he sees it. Let me explain.

According to 2 Corinthians 10, strongholds have a lot to do with imaginations. This is significant because in the Greek, the root word from which the word imagination is translated is logos, which of course is defined as a word. This means that an imagination is more than an image we see; instead, it is a word we hear that transmits on the frequency of thought. In other words, there are spirits speaking in the atmosphere, and their goal is to make their words sound like our thoughts.

All of our thoughts are not always our own thoughts. When the enemy wants to establish a stronghold, he begins to speak words in the atmosphere. When this takes place, we do not necessarily hear what is being said; however, the words are being transmitted into our minds as thoughts and ideas and being reinforced by images. Therefore, everything I have written leads back to the following point concerning how principalities and powers operate.

Media and mass communications are the primary means in our day and time concerning how culture is created. They have the ability to take thoughts and ideas and communicate them via sound and images. This is significant because what we hear and see will ultimately determine our thoughts and our actions the most. This is because our eyes and ears are access points into our hearts. In fact, what we see and hear even has the ability to impact our moral clarity at its core.

We should, therefore, be careful what we allow to feed our minds because the enemy will often deploy tactics in the media to propagate a certain demonic agenda. Music, arts, entertainment, and people of influence often play a big role in this effort. These mediums are used strategically to establish strongholds in atmospheres over cities, regions, and nations.

Furthermore, we have to understand that apart from the power of the air, media couldn't even exist, which lands us back at Ephesians 2. The things communicated through media are merely thoughts reinforced by sound and images. They are merely frequencies traveling on airwaves.

We should not underestimate the power and science

of the activity that takes place within spiritual atmospheres. Science has proven that words, pictures, music, and even smells affect our moods, thoughts, and attitudes.

Those thoughts and moods then create auras, which are vibrations, signals, and frequencies that give off waves of energy to attract a match. In other words, we are created by God to embrace what we see and hear, and ultimately attract those things into our lives. If we don't understand this reality, the enemy will take advantage of it every time and utilize this reality in order to gain the upper hand in the battle.

Demonic Targets Continued ...

It is very important that you realize that understanding demonic targets should not cause us to become battle-paranoid. Neither should we assume that some of the struggles we encounter in life are an automatic result of demonic attack. We should also always remember that the mentioned targets are corporate and not personal.

I want to reiterate that demonic ranks have specific targets, and most of the time, they have little interest in attacking our personal lives individually. However, when demonic ranks hit their actual specific targets, it affects specific areas of our lives and we feel the heat of the battle. James 1 will help us understand this truth.

James 1:2 states, "when you fall into divers trials..."

I want to emphasize the word divers in James 1, which means diversities. The truth is that the mentioning of diversities of trials in James 1 should be a revelation to us that every struggle is not the same. Therefore, we have to properly interpret the struggle in our lives so that we can discern both the intended purpose of God in the struggle and the way God intends for us to respond to it.

We Must Properly Interpret the Conflict

One of the first revelations that will help you become more effective in spiritual battle is to understand that every struggle you deal with is not the devil. Sometimes we just have trials to go through. Other times there is a level of friction required in our lives because we are travailing and almost at the point of birthing. Sometimes we are going through things because of past decisions, but no matter what we are going through, there is power to overcome it if we respond properly.

Many of us enter into spiritual battle inappropriately or prematurely because we are not properly discerning the nature of the struggle in our lives. If we wrongly diagnose the problem, we will likewise wrongly prescribe the solution. Truth is we don't overcome every struggle the same way.

We must properly assess the struggle in order to begin walking out the biblical application for victory in that particular area of struggle. Most importantly, we must be careful that the way we respond to a trial and attempt to engage in spiritual battle does not attract a demonic warfare that God never intended for us to fight. I recommend the book *Needless Casualties of War* by John Paul Jackson for more understanding in this area.

Sometimes, because of the heat of the battle, there are certain struggles in our lives that surface that are not necessarily in direct relation to a personal demonic confrontation. However, many believers retaliate against demonic forces in the heat of the battle, thinking that they are effectively binding demons—and in reality, they are not

104

even touching them. If we are going to effectively target our enemy and take him out, we must learn his targets so that we can beat him to the punch (what you learned in this chapter). We must also learn how to biblically and strategically deal with demonic powers in ways that do not attract unnecessary demonic retaliation.

Chapter 11

Wrestling Principalities

Chapter Objectives:
- Learn basics on how to strategically deal with principalities and powers.
- Learn three basic and strategic warfare prayers.
- Learn why the prayer of agreement is key in spiritual warfare prayers and much more.

Basics on How to Deal With Demonic Powers

The knowledge and revelation that has been made available to you in this book, specifically concerning the battle at hand, should be evidence to you that the way we war must change. Once you understand the truths we have covered up to this point, it becomes easy to discern why many have only attracted more warfare because of the ways that they have attempted to engage the battle. If principalities really operate in the ways that we have examined, we would have to conclude that we must become both more realistic and strategic in our approach to the battle.

The issue at hand is that there is little biblical support for how many attempt to engage in spiritual warfare. Therefore, it would be very foolish to learn all we have learned about Ephesians 6:12 and continue to do battle the way we have always done it. We obviously need to reconsider our effectiveness in what we consider as spiritual warfare and intercession.

In other words, your response to all you have learned about the demonic should not be an attempt to take them on in spiritual combat. In fact, there is no scripture that validates the notion that we are even called to address principalities and powers in prayer the way that many assume. We are, rather, called to war against them in ways that strategically wrestle them down, which is an art that requires great skill and should never be attempted alone or apart from proper accountability to church leadership and a clear leading of the Holy Ghost.

The truth is that in addition to Ephesians 6:12, the only other scripture that directly references how to actually deal with demonic principalities and powers is Ephesians 3:10. However, there are many scriptures that can support how to execute Ephesian 3:10. We will examine all of that in more detail in the chapter on "How to Bind and Loose." For now, however, I couldn't reiterate enough how—based on what we have learned about principalities, their core operations, and their key battle targets—there is no reason that we should continue to engage in faulty assumptions of intercession.

Three Strategic Prayers in Opposing Principalities and Powers

I want to remind you of the very first truth that we covered as we began our journey in the art of war. And that is how warfare prayer is strategic in nature. Therefore, based on what we have come to understand of what principalities and powers target so far, there are strategic prayers that we can pray in order to cripple them without attracting unnecessary retaliation. The following three strategic prayers are my personal recommendations in applying this wisdom.

Jonathan Ferguson

However, before we deal with the following three prayers, I want to "tease" you with the revelation that the prayer of repentance is one of the most strategic prayers that we can pray in warfare. And yes, I know it's teasing you because that's all I'm going to write about that right now.

But don't worry, I'm going to explain how repentance is strategic in more detail in the chapter on Binding and Loosing. For now, I only want to cover three strategic prayers in reference to praying in ways to dismantle the demonic agendas of principalities and powers that we have previously examined.

NOTE: The following prayers are only examples and are not included in the prayer index found in chapter twenty.

Three Strategic Prayers...

1) Claim your seat of authority

Example Prayer

Father, I thank you that you have seated us in heavenly places with Christ Jesus according to Ephesians 2:6. And because we are seated with Jesus, we are seated far above principalities and powers according to Ephesians 1:20-21. You said in your Word that you will take the poor and set them among princes in 1 Samuel 2:1-10. So now I thank you that you are taking people with no influence and giving them influence because of where you are sitting them in the realm of the Spirit in Jesus name. And right now, I claim that seat of authority in the realm of the spirit. I receive a new power for affluence and influence in order to make a greater impact for your kingdom in every region and territory that you see fit.

The Instruction

Now notice that nothing in the prayer suggests that we are attempting to "dethrone ancient demons." Neither does the prayer suggest that we "bind all of the demonic powers seated on thrones" over various nations and geographical areas. The prayer is revelatory, and it is addressed toward God as opposed to spewing railing accusations that could attract demonic backlash (Jude 6).

The Revelation

It is not those who claim the thrones in the earth, but it is those who claim the thrones in the spirit who have a ruling voice and governing influence in this world. For some, the thought that we can assume a throne in the realm of the spirit may seem far stretched. However, it is a scripturally confirmed reality.

Despite the controversy, Daniel 7 teaches that God showed Daniel in a vision multiple thrones that were suspended in the atmosphere. This means that there are other thrones created by God other than the throne of God. In fact, Colossians 1 teaches that in and through Christ, there are many thrones that were created. Lastly, Ephesians 2:6 teaches that we are seated in heavenly places in Christ.

The significance concerning claiming our seats of authority is in the fact that principalities and powers rank lower than the thrones that we have assumed in Christ. According to Ephesians 1:20-22 and Ephesians 2:5-6, they are under our feet and they have become our footstool. We will explain this in more detail in the chapter entitled "Taking the High Places."

2) Ask for power in the air

Example Prayer

Father, I pray in Jesus name that you shift the powers of the air, and that you cause the atmosphere of your presence and power to overshadow cities, regions, and nations.

The Instruction

Now notice that the prayer does not suggest that we bind every demonic power that is operating in the air. Neither are we binding the prince of the power of the air that functions in various territories. We are again addressing God and not the devil, and we are simply asking that the atmosphere of His presence and power overshadow the cities, regions, and nations that we may find ourselves praying over. When this happens, the demonic powers of the air are overpowered by the atmosphere of God's presence.

The Revelation

We need atmospheres of God's presence and power to invade whole nations in ways where people experience the reality of Jesus. Although there are demonic powers of the air (Ephesians 2:1-2), the kingdom of God brings an atmosphere in the Holy Ghost according to Romans 14:17. We can shift demonic powers and atmospheres and seize the power of the air through prayer.

3) Command the opening of the gates and doors

Example Prayer

Father, in Jesus name, open up the ancient gates and the everlasting doors and come in as the King of Glory according to Psalm 24:6-10. Come into our space mighty to save and mighty to deliver. Let great and effectual doors be opened so that a word is spoken that advances your kingdom in the earth according to 1 Corinthians 16:9 and Colossians 4:3.

The Instruction

Now notice that the prayer is not focused on kicking every demonic spirit out of the city. Neither are we attempting to bind the prince of Persia or any other demonic spirit that we claim we discern to be the ruling principality over a given territory. We are addressing our heavenly Father and asking Him to open up regions spiritually for the kingdom of God to advance and expand therein.

The Revelation
There are either angels or demons that guard the gates that grant access into territories, influence, prominence, etc.

Remember:
- Prince of Persia (Daniel 10:13)
- Ezekiel and angels with charge over city (Ezekiel 9:1-4)

Just as there are tolls in certain states that must be paid prior to entering certain territories, there are likewise certain gates we must pass through in the spirit before we can come into promotion or advance and take more ground for the kingdom of God. It is a spiritual principle and only spiritual people understand it. Sometimes the most strategic prayer we can pray in battle against territorial spirits is to ask for the gates or to make declarations, like David did in Psalm 24, inviting the King of Glory to come in at the gates.

Spiritual Mapping and Beyond

As we conclude this first prayer focus with basic principles on how to deal with principalities and powers, I want to reiterate the importance of counting the cost and examining the preliminaries of battle in order to ensure victory. Proverbs 21:22 confirms this truth as it teaches that a wise man thoroughly investigates a city in order to overthrow the confidence of the mighty men within it. The way that many implement this in prayer is called spiritual mapping.

It is in spiritual mapping that the type of thorough investigation necessary in uprooting demonic powers in a land takes place. It is a process that includes the journaling of various examinations of a territory's historical activities that inspired its current spiritual climate. It is no different than how Moses sent out spies to scout the land of Canaan that the nation of Israel was preparing to conquest in the book of Numbers.

Adequate research is needed, and certain logistics are to be examined in order to pinpoint what strongholds the enemy has established. The wisdom in this is that if we are going to claim a territory, it will require that we eventually deal with the level of demonic activity rooted in the demographics of its culture. Some of the things to research include:

- History, trends, and cultural influences (statistics)
- Traditions; customs; religious backgrounds/beliefs; family, city & nation origins; moral standards; music; hobbies; crime and its nature; economy; education, etc.

We should utilize RESOURCES such as Google search, libraries, and research development teams to help direct research and assessments. Also, *Possessing the Gates of the Enemy* by Cindy Jacobs is another great resource among many other books that will help us understand this concept of spiritual mapping.

However, if all we do is spiritually map how demons are working in various territories, but we do not discern how God is moving in those same territories, we defeat the purpose. If we are not careful, we will put more emphasis on the demonic in our cities than what is healthy in the context of maintaining a healthy and Godly perspective of our land. And therein lies the faultiness of the majority of our spiritual warfare prayers.

It is possible to become so overly focused on exposing the demonic that our prayers seem to almost conjure demons instead of defeat them. In fact, it is sad that many know more names of demons than they know about the power of Jesus. The truth is that we should be more focused on the majesty and power that God is revealing in our geographical locations as we pray and not the demons that we are in war against.

This is why the way that Jesus and the early church dealt with the demonic was by advancing the kingdom of God in the earth. The concept does not refute the need for us to understand the army that we are opposing, but it does give us a pattern concerning how we should direct our focus. I don't want to go into specifics about this now, but be sure that we are going to examine this war tactic in more detail in the chapter "Recover All."

The Power of Agreement in Warfare Prayer

The last thing that I want to leave you with, in reference to how to effectively deal with demonic principalities and powers, is the importance of utilizing the prayer of agreement. We have to understand that dealing with this level of demonic activity will require that we do not attempt to rage into the battle alone. In conclusion of this chapter, I want to take a moment and inspire you concerning the power of agreement in prayer.

The Minority and The Majority

If we take a close look at Proverbs 14:28, it teaches us that the ability for principalities to remain established relies upon the sway of the majority. This means that when a prince demon is seeking to establish its jurisdiction, the demon understands that the more people it can get to come into agreement—the more authority it can attempt to usurp in a particular territory. This is why a prince demon works so hard in establishing strongholds that eventually become the prevailing opinions of a particular culture.

One of the ways that principalities rally their campaigns is that they basically look for people in positions of influence who will buy into their ideology. The demon understands that if they can succeed in seducing those in authority, the majority of the population that it is seeking to dominate will then follow ignorantly in suit. Therefore, we have to understand that in reality, there are people that support demonic agendas both intentionally and unintentionally.

Good news is, however, that although the power of a prince relies upon the sway of the majority, we are working with a far greater power (agreement) and a far greater strategist in war tactics in prayer (Jesus). The truth is that our authority supersedes the majority vote because of the power of agreement in prayer. Deuteronomy 32:30 gives us revelation into this reality when it speaks of how one can chase a thousand, and yet, two could chase ten thousand.

We have to understand that if two can chase ten thousand, the revelation is that when we pray in agreement, our prayers take on the force of an army. Therefore, in dealing with principalities and powers, we must utilize the power of agreement, even if they're only two or three that comply. The reality is that the vast majority does not have to be in agreement with what God wants to do in the earth. Only the ones that are in compliance with God need to link up in prayer, even if they're only a few of them.

Jesus said that wherever two or three are gathered in prayer, He would be there in the midst. The revelation is that when you add Jesus to the minority, the opposition of the majority becomes irrelevant. The power of agreement that can be activated with just two or three in prayer outweighs the majority vote in the realm of the spirit.

When we pray in the power of agreement, we are partnering with the Lord Jesus and allowing Him to work things the way He knows best. Afterwards, we must simply align with the Lord and follow His plan of action. And if so, He can use even a small remnant to see cultures, nations, and generations transformed.

When we pray in agreement, we have to embrace the reality that we are no longer doing the fighting, but the Lord Himself will fight our battles. This is why the prayer of agreement is so powerful in spiritual warfare tactics. It literally releases a power that is beyond our personal strength in the battle. It causes us to become more aware of the fact that Jesus Himself is fighting for us. Therefore, the next prayer focus in the art of war is that the Lord's victory be enforced.

Closing Word

Sometimes we focus so much on the warfare that we forget who is fighting for us and what type of reinforcement that brings. Truth is that God is fighting for us and He is on our side. You must not ever forget this because it is very possible to become so knowledgeable in battle tactics that you begin fighting battles that you were never meant to fight. Jesus is the one leading in the battle—not us (Exodus 15:3; Joshua 5:15).

This means if you want to know the best way to effectively deal with principalities and powers ... it is to let Jesus Himself deal with them. They are no match for Him. Whatever demonic ranks there may be that have set themselves up in your nation or your city, you have to know that they must bow their knees to Jesus, which brings me to my closing point.

In addition to repentance, the prayers of praise and worship are some of the most powerful and strategic warfare prayers that we could ever pray. When Jesus is exalted, his enemies have no choice but to be scattered. If you do not know and embrace the truth of that, you are wasting your time trying to make demons subject themselves to your commands.

It is important to bring these things into perspective due to how much I've written to expose the demonic ranks. I want to make sure that we are clear on this one thing, which is how this book is not written to emphasize the battle more than it is to emphasize the victory that we already have in the battle, and how to implement that victory. The remaining prayer focuses will emphasize just that—now that we have this foundation laid.

Chapter 12

Jesus, Our War General

Chapter Objectives

- Realize that Jesus has sovereignty in the battle and the importance of submitting to that reality.
- Learn why warfare prayers should address God more than they address the enemy.
- Learn why it is important to have a battle plan, and never engage war without a clear directive from the Lord, and much more.

I want to context the next two prayer focuses in the thought and idea of Jesus being our war general. In doing so, it will fix our perspective on the sovereignty of God in the battle. What I mean by this is that Jesus is the one calling the shots in the warfare, not us. It is only as we forget this principle that we enter into unauthorized practices of spiritual battle.

Prayer focus #2 in the Art of War

The second prayer focus in the art of war is that the Lord's victory is enforced. The reason that we are to pray that the Lord enforces His victory is because we must remember that it is the Lord that fights the battle. In fact, we should never attempt to go into a spiritual battle without the revelation that the victory is already won.

The truth is that there are levels of victory that can come in our lives in prayer before we ever have to enter into strategic levels of warfare. The very essence of such prayers is echoed all throughout the books of Psalms. In fact, reading the books of Psalms has completely revolutionized my perspective of spiritual warfare prayer.

If we will remember that God is fighting our battles and petition Him for the victory that He has already wrought, we will learn that there are some demonic enemies we will never have to rebuke, bind, etc. My experience in this revelation came in a season in which the Lord had me journal all of the warfare prayers in the books of Psalms that consisted of specific petitions of various psalmists to God concerning their enemies. I noticed that these were powerful prayers that are symbolic of how we should pray to God concerning our spiritual enemies.

I also noticed that the prayers in Psalms were directed towards God and they were not prayed to address the enemy directly. It is a rather different concept of what we consider warfare prayer to be in our current culture. However, it was revealed to me that there are certain prayers that we can pray to God concerning victory in the battle that will cause us to overcome demonic warfare prior to ever having to address the enemy.

I realized that these prayers will not only provide proper covering prior to confronting demonic forces, but will also prevent us from entering into levels of warfare prematurely that we are not properly prepared to engage. This concept in warfare helps us to remember that it is God fighting our battles, and it is God that gives us the victory. It helps us remember that the weapons of our warfare are only mighty "through God," ultimately causing us to forever embrace that it is not by might nor by power but "by my Spirit says the Lord."(Be sure to reference these warfare prayers in the prayer index section of this book, by the way).

I want to reiterate that if we learn to keep in mind the reality of how Jesus is the leading commanding officer in whatever battles we face, it would help prevent us from taking the fight into our own hands. It is only as we attempt to war in our own ability and wisdom that we experience casualties of war. We have to embrace the fact that it is only as we engage the battle in ways that our general commands that we experience the victory in prayer that we desire, which leads to our third prayer focus.

Prayer focus #3 in the Art of War

The third prayer focus in the art of war is to ask the Lord for a battle plan. You will find this prayer focus is rather simple to understand and notice that it does not require an exhaustive explanation. Basically, Proverbs 24:5-6 confirms the truth of this prayer effort as it teaches that we are not to go into war apart from counsel. And it not only teaches that it is wise to have a battle plan, but also that the counsel will result in our safety.

War is strategy

Many approach spiritual warfare as if they are out to get the devil back for every wrong caused in their lives—not understanding that warfare is not retaliation, but rather strategy. In fact, I want to reiterate that the word war, in 2 Corinthians 10:3, comes from a Greek word from which we get the word strategy. And it is only as we progressively follow the Lord's strategy that we effectively combat and overthrow demonic powers (Luke 10:17), little by little (Deuteronomy 7:22).

In 1 Corinthians 9:26, Paul mentions two things that I believe are critical in understanding the effectiveness in having a spiritual battle plan. The first thing that Paul mentions is how when he wars, he does not merely fight the air. In other words, he is very strategic in the way that he engages the battle to be sure that he actually effectively lands a strike to his intended target.

119

The second thing that Paul mentions in 1 Corinthians 9 is how he buffets himself, which has a lot to do with self-control. The truth is that if we do not have self-control, we are already defeated and don't even know it. Could you imagine an army full of individuals who lacked self-control? They would have the potential to create complete chaos. We are the same way in the realm of the spirit when we are not disciplined enough to become strategic in the way we battle.

According to 1 Samuel 30:8, before David went into battle, he asked the Lord if he should pursue. The text demonstrates how we must likewise ask for strategy in battle and become careful to obey the Lord's instruction. Even Jesus Himself did not go around picking fights with the devil, but rather the Spirit led Him into a wilderness where He overcame the devil (Matthew 4:1-11).

We must learn from the example of Jesus, and never go into warfare unless we have clear leading of His Spirit concerning how to do so. Although this is one of the most ignored aspects of spiritual warfare, it is one that would prevent many of the casualties and hardships that result from bad battle tactics. The truth is that there is a specific target that we are called to take out. Therefore, when God gives victory, He does not merely give us spiritual weapons, but He gives us counsel and wisdom. It is our job to have enough discipline to wait on the Lord's strategy and then obey it.

Chapter 13

Taking the High Places

Chapter Objectives:
- Understand what the High place represents.
- Embrace spiritual protocol and understand your authority in Christ.
- Understand why it is important to both live in the Spirit and understand the Spiritual realm.
- Learn how to remain on the offensive in battle instead of the defensive.

Prayer focus #4 in the Art of War

The fourth prayer focus in the art of war is to actually engage the battle. What I mean by this is to pursue, attack, and overtake your enemies. In fact, one of the most empowering revelations concerning spiritual warfare is that we can execute vengeance upon our adversaries according to Psalm 149:9. This means that we can literally inflict pain upon demonic powers in the realm of the spirit. This is one reason why when Jesus dealt with demons, they would be in fear of His torment.

Our spiritual warfare is not merely symbolic. There is a real battle going on in the spirit world, and there are war casualties that come with it. Furthermore, now that you know what level you are fighting on, the victory is being enforced, and you have a battle plan; it is not only time to pursue, attack, and overtake, but it is also time to plunder your enemy.

The connotation in plundering is that we not only defeat our enemy, but that we secure and confiscate all of his goods and substance to be enjoyed at our own leisure and utilized for the advancement of our Kingdom. Therefore, there are many factors that I'm going to teach you in how to successfully attack and plunder your enemies over the next couple of chapters because I believe you are now ready to engage the battle. But first, let's lay a couple more foundations that will help us properly engage the battle.

The Lord spoke to me and said:
"Many talk about spiritual warfare but do not understand the spiritual realm that the warfare takes place in."

There are three main hindrances to people understanding how to properly engage the warfare that Ephesians 6:12 mentions as follows:

1) Not knowing what Ephesians 6:12 is actually saying. (Note: For those of you reading this book, however, you no longer have that problem because we have taken the time in Chapter 9 to define the demonic ranks that Paul makes mention of.)

2) Knowing more about the warfare of Ephesians 6:12 than we know about the victory that we already have over the warfare.

3) Not understanding the spirit realm and its protocol. (We have to understand that when Paul wrote Ephesians 6, he was not giving a theory, but he had seen into the realm in which the hierarchy mentioned was established.)

The first hindrance is obvious. We will focus on the second hindrance later, but for now, out of the previous three, not understanding the spirit realm is the main hindrance we encounter as we enter our next phase of engaging in battle. The truth is that we can't just go into the spirit realm doing anything we want to do when we want to do it; there is a protocol. In fact, we can actually be unknowingly doing things that sabotage the victory if we do not understand the spirit realm, our place and protocol within it, and the nature of the battle within it.

Understanding Spiritual Protocol

One primary protocol of the spirit realm is that in order to understand or go into the spirit realm, you have to first be welcomed or invited in. For example, Ezekiel had angelic escorts that carried him into the realm of the spirit to show him the visions of God throughout the entirety of his prophetic writings. And don't forget about John, the apostle, who heard a voice in the book of Revelations telling him to come up higher so that he could know the revelation of future events. Whether it was Ezekiel or John, Old or New Testament, no one entered the realm of the spirit prior to the invitation.

And as it was for Ezekiel, John, and many other biblical examples, so it is with us. We have been invited by the King to know Him and have access in His world, which is the Spirit realm. In fact, the story of how Esther took a risk in presenting herself to the king is another great example of the fundamental truth of all spiritual protocol. It is powerful because although Esther feared that she would break protocol, she had to rely on her relationship with the king in hopes of favor being extended to her.

Simply put, Esther's story is a great illustration of how a relationship with the Lord is highest priority and protocol in learning the realm of the Spirit. The logic is that you can't know the spirit realm without knowing the Spirit of the spirit realm. However, it's sad that some know more about spiritual warfare than they know about Jesus. Truth is, many live in defeat because they either do not know the Lord or have not accepted His invitation to enter into a higher dimension of living life in the supernatural. Our invitation is that we have been seated in heavenly places where all of the blessings of God are made available to us according to Ephesians 2:6 and Ephesians 1:3.

Our Invitation, Access, & Authority in High Places

Before we go any further, we have to embrace the fact that Ephesians 2:6 is an invitation into the spiritual realm. Let me explain. The truth is that although my spirit is seated in Christ in the high places, I'm still living here on earth in my body. Therefore, the revelation of Ephesians 2:6 is an invitation because I have a choice. I can either operate in the natural or I can operate in the supernatural.

Why is this important?

According to Ephesians 1:3, the blessings are in the spiritual realm. That means I must first get into the spiritual realm if I am going to experience the blessings that are there. In fact, the blessings that Ephesians 1:3 speaks of are not trivial. They are the very reality that we have a bible full of benefits that belong to us because of the victory that Jesus accomplished at the cross to disarm every demonic principality and power that would seek to undermine and frustrate the manifestation of those benefits.

We also have to know, according to Ephesians 2:6, that because of our positioning in Jesus in high places, demonic principalities and powers do not operate above our heads but under our feet. Jesus did not only disarm them, but He also sat above them, which means that we are also seated above them (Ephesians 1:20; 2:6). This means that we not only already have the victory, but we have the advantage, which I will explain more momentarily. For now, we have to be clear on the fact that we are not fighting for the victory, but we are fighting with the victory.

Therefore, when our circumstances do not reflect the victory, we have to learn how to operate from our position in the Spirit realm in order to enforce that victory. This is what I call *taking the high places*. And it is what we must do first in this next phase of engaging the spiritual battle.

Keep in mind as we go further that the concepts that you are learning are not mere theories. I have noticed that there is no singular scripture on spiritual warfare that is remotely complete in thought. Therefore, the revelation requires you to interpret scripture with scripture.

There are many scriptures that are taken into consideration when forming these concepts. I pray that you are not merely reading through the book, but rather dissecting the scriptural references in order to see why these concepts are necessary to understand in order to engage spiritual battle both safely and correctly.

Taking the High Places

In ancient times, among all of the preferred battlegrounds in dealing with the art of war, the highest ground was the greatest vantage point of all in the battle. If we are going to truly understand the battle we are in, we must first understand the vantage point we've been given in the battle. And understanding our vantage point has to do with understanding the high places that we are called to assume.

Jonathan Ferguson

Understanding the High Places

I want to reiterate that the high places are in reference to the spirit realm. They are various spiritual dimensions that we have access to through Christ. We are called to live and walk in the Spirit so that what already belongs to us in the Spirit can manifest in the earth.

We have also previously mentioned how principalities and powers operate in high places, which means that our battle is in the spiritual realm. However, it's time we go deeper in our understanding. It is at this place that we are now beginning to further embrace that our advantage over principalities is also in the high places.

Now let me explain this before many attempt to apply this in warfare and get into a lot of trouble spiritually. Many run with an incomplete revelation of the spiritual battles being waged and attempt to take on demonic powers and end up with serious war casualties in their lives. The truth is our advantage over principalities does not give us this license to necessarily confront them in battle, especially apart from the proper strategies of the Holy Spirit in order to do so.

For now, I simply want you to understand that demonic powers only have the advantage as long as we are not operating in and by the Spirit of God. Our victory is already won in the supernatural dimension. Jesus has already defeated our foes, and we are seated in Him far above them.

It is only as we develop our relationship with the Lord and receive the word of God that we accept our invitation into the spiritual dimension where the victory already belongs to us. And it is the word of God that acts as the law and protocol of that dimension. Learning and embracing these realities play a big role in how we live and

126

walk in the Spirit.

Living in the Spirit is living in the Victory

Living in the Spirit is about living by faith, and faith in fact comes by hearing, and hearing by the word of God. Hebrews 11 teaches that by faith Enoch walked with God, which means that he lived and walked in the Spirit as if he would in the natural. I believe that this is exactly what Peter did when he walked on the water. He was actually walking in another dimension because of how the word of God gives us access to another dimension.

When Jesus said, "Come," Peter walked on that word and not just on the water. Likewise, it is said that Samuel's words did not fall to the ground in 1 Samuel 3:19. In other words, he spoke in another dimension.

The word of God is what takes us to another dimension and gives us the knowledge and understanding of the high places we have been given access to in Christ. Whenever God takes us to another dimension, He teaches us about that dimension. You have to understand the dimension God has taken you to or you will forfeit some things that God has already given you access to enjoy.

In fact, most of the warfare we think we are in at times would become irrelevant if we understood the high places we have access to in Christ Jesus. This means that most of our problems are revelation problems. And the real problem is that we have not taken the time to understand and claim our kingdom citizenship and rights. This is why Ephesians 3:11-20 teaches that God will do more than we can ask or think in our lives if we allow Him to give us a thorough comprehension of what belongs to us.

So Where Does the Warfare Begin?

According to 2 Corinthians 2:11, ignorance is one of the main reasons that the enemy finds opportunity to take advantage over us. We do not perish because the enemy is more powerful than us, but we perish for the lack of knowledge. In other words, when we don't know our word, we give the enemy home court advantage in the battle. This should never be. Ephesians 4:27 instructs us to give no place to the enemy. And in the context of us being warriors, this means that we should never allow the enemy to deceive us into fighting on his level and on his terms.

The truth is that there are many conditions in life that attempt to have us distracted by what we are experiencing in the natural, instead of enforcing the reality of what already belongs to us in the supernatural. This means that giving our problems more attention than the promises of God can give the enemy just as much an advantage over us as ignorance of the word of God does. However, we have to come to a place where we understand that the promises of God are more powerful than any circumstance that seems contrary. And in order to do so, we have to learn how to pray from our POSITION instead of praying about our CONDITION. Let me explain.

Condition vs. Position

Ephesians 2:6 + Ephesians 1:20-22 = we are seated in Christ in heavenly places far above principality and power.

Our position is that we are seated above what we are warring and praying against. This means we have the advantage in spiritual battle, which means that when we pray, we should be praying the solution and not the problem. Our condition is often that because we do not understand our position, we end up fighting on the defensive instead of the offensive in the battle. Selah.

Our condition says that we are in a struggle, but our position says that we have already overcome it. Our condition suggests to us that we are victims of the enemy's attack, but our position reminds us that demonic powers are already under our feet.

If we allow our condition to pressure us in retaliation against the enemy, in the name of so-called spiritual warfare, we can forfeit our advantage. And it is only when we forfeit our advantage that we find ourselves fighting on the defensive instead of the offensive in battle.

Fighting on the offense instead of the defense

Let me help you understand what I mean by fighting on the offensive. Don't misinterpret me. I'm not in any way implying that being on the offensive in battle gives us any license to run into battles presumptuously that we are not authorized to be in by our Commander and Chief, Jesus. I'm sure at this point you have embraced the importance of never engaging a battle that the Lord has not clearly instructed you in because we have already previously examined that truth in detail.

However, in order to understand what it means to be on the offensive, there are two biblical concepts of warfare that I want you to examine. The first thing that I want you to understand is what it means to stand according to Ephesians 6:14. And the next thing that I want you to understand is what it means to tread according to Deuteronomy 11:24 and Luke 10:19.

Standing

Many read Ephesians 6:14 and completely miss the

revelation, not understanding the historical significance in the writing. The truth is that standing in battle means a lot less to us than it did to those who originally embraced the KJV translation of the text. Therefore, lets briefly take a moment to understand the text, specifically from an Old English perspective. It is significant because the translators chose to use a word that culturally represented a more offensive, aggressive approach as opposed to a passive approach to the battle. Let me explain.

Historically, in the mind of an old English soldier, to stand literally meant to be the last one standing victoriously after battle. It did not mean to merely endure the onslaughts and defensively resist the aggressive attacks of the enemy. And it did not mean to just "hang on in there" after you've done all you could do. Contrary to popular opinion—to stand meant to conquer and to plunder the enemy.

More specifically, it meant to pursue and overtake the opposing army until you were the last standing. Let me make this a little plainer. It meant slaughter everything in your path, take no prisoners, let none escape, and show no mercy. It meant that after you have done all you know to do, your enemies will fall and you will be the last standing in the battle. And this is the attitude we must take when we read Ephesians 6 as it tells us to stand, and this leads to our next word, which is *treading*.

Treading

According to Deuteronomy 11:24, the revelation of treading is beyond walking land and claiming territory. Treading, by definition, is a militant army invasion. It is a forward conquest designed to cripple the opposing army with fear.

It is no coincidence that Jesus uses this same

130

terminology when explaining to the disciples their authority over devils. The truth is that demons and devils literally trembled and feared the disciples, and the reason why is found in Deuteronomy 11:24 when God tells Moses to tread. The revelation is in the fact that God did not only promise He would give them the land in Deuteronomy, but also that their enemies would fear them as they would move forward and tread that land.

In Luke 10:19, when Jesus told the disciples that they had power to tread, He was in part telling them that their authority was in their forward movement. This means that as long as we are moving forward, demons can't help but to fear us. In fact, the reason that the enemy wants us on the defensive is because he fears our forward movement. The truth is that as long as we are offensively treading, the enemy has no choice but to tremble in fear of us.

Another interesting thing to note concerning treading is that a "treader" was also defined as an archer. This is significant because an archer is a person who is skilled with the bow and arrow and trained to hit targets. They would be equivalent to professional snipers.

A treader's job is to target an enemy, find a vantage point, and then take out the targeted enemy. This is what happened to Goliath when David defeated him with one strike to the head. It is obvious to us that David's stone hit the target that he intended. He hit the bull's eye, and I prophesy that God is yet raising up those who will become spiritual snipers and take out giants just as David took out Goliath.

Experts at War

Treaders are experts at war. They are not mere freedom fighters or vigilantes. They are qualified warriors assigned to a specific task with a specific set of skills and abilities.

For example, as we have examined the ranks of principalities and powers, we should also consider that understanding their order is equivalent to understanding the difference between the marines, the navy, the air force, and the army. It would be foolish to send the marines against the air force, or to send an army against the navy. Why? Because not only is there a specific strategy for each battle, but there is a specific military tactical unit that is assigned to fight on specific terrains that other military units are not.

The army is not assigned to the waters just as the navy is not assigned to do battle in the air. It is no different than how in ancient civilizations there were troops who were trained to fight on mountaintops while others were trained to fight in valleys. There were also those who were trained to battle in swamps as opposed to those who trained to fight in deserts.

Likewise, there are different spiritual terrains that various battles can be waged on. Some will be valleys and some hills, but when we are skillful in strategic offensive battle prayers, we know the climatic conditions surrounding the battle and how to shift them. However, it is only from our seated position in Christ that we can discern the spiritual atmosphere, shift it, and in turn bring the battle to our grounds and on our terms.

The crooked places can be made straight. The rough places can be made smooth. The valleys can be exalted and mountains can be removed. We will explain this more in the chapter entitled "Secrets of War."

Special Task Forces

We have to see ourselves as a special task force unit within God's army with a specific assigned effort in the battle, no different than the marines, air force, or any other military branch. And we have to know that the spiritual terrains, which our military unit has been assigned to, afford us the greatest advantage. What am I saying? I'm saying that we are seated in heavenly places where principalities and powers are under our feet. We have an awesome vantage point in the battle in which we already have the victory.

Therefore, we have to be strategic in the way we battle, and if you have made it to this point, that is exactly what you are ready to learn and exactly what the Lord is ready to show you. Now you are ready to learn how to effectively engage in strategic warfare prayers that bind and loose ... and as you do, you manifest the victory that is already given to us in Christ Jesus.

Chapter 14

Binding and Loosing

Chapter Objectives:
- Understand the difference between binding and loosing in the contexts of prayer and deliverance.
- Understand the legalities of binding and loosing.
- Understand why praying strategically is key in your ability to effectively bind and loose.
- Understand why repentance is a key battle strategy and much more.

There are spiritual legalities that are to be considered when dealing with the conflict at hand. And, I reiterate, a mere attempt in taunting devils in our prayers will not suffice in seeing any real victories.

If our prayers are going to be the weapons that effectively remove demonic strongholds, we must learn how to pray in ways that bind and loose. However, binding and loosing are in no way, shape, form, or fashion the totality of the spiritual battle being waged. They are in actuality only part of the full picture. You are going to learn more about what I mean by this as you go throughout this chapter.

Binding & Loosing What's Already Bound & Loosed

One of the first key principles we should understand of the subject at hand is what the scripture is actually saying when it speaks of binding and loosing in Matthew 16:19. Most understand the scripture to mean that whatever we bind and loose in the earth will be bound and loosed in heaven. However, the correct translation of the scripture actually says that we should bind and loose what is already bound and loosed in heaven, and not the other way around.

So in reality, heaven doesn't bind and loose whatever we bind and loose, but we must bind and loose what heaven has already bound and loosed. Therefore, it is impossible to effectively bind and loose if we do not know what heaven has already bound and loosed. This means that one of the first objectives in becoming effective in this effort is to get into the word of God in order to know everything that should and should not be a part of our lives.

Only in knowing God's word will we know what is already bound and loosed in heaven. And then, if we will bind and loose what has already been bound and loosed, heaven will reinforce us, which is what Matthew 16:19 more accurately conveys.

I know this may be a rather different approach to many who are familiar with the subject of binding and loosing. But if you stay with me, your prayer life will never be the same.

Binding the Strongman

We have to understand that when Jesus mentioned binding and loosing in scripture, He did so in two completely different contexts. In one context, binding and loosing was in reference to the ministry of deliverance according to Mark 12:29 and Luke 11:22. However, in another context, binding and loosing was rather taught in reference to legislating heaven's laws in the earth through prayer according to Matthew 16:19.

Our issue, when it comes to binding and loosing in

prayer, is that there is often mixture in what we have learned of deliverance pertaining to binding and loosing, and how we attempt to navigate in prayer pertaining to binding and loosing. The confusion comes in when we are without thorough understanding in the matter at hand. But I want to take the time to clear the misconception.

However, in order to do so, I only want to deal with binding and loosing in the context of prayer. Therefore, whatever you have learned about the subject in context of deliverance will most often not apply to what you will learn as you continue to read.

This means that we must embrace that there are many effective concepts of what it means to bind and loose, in addition to what it represents in a context of deliverance ministry. Even pertaining to prayer, there may be many other intercessory prayer books that may emphasize different aspects of binding and loosing that will not be examined in this book. And it's not that the information is necessarily conflicting, but it may in fact be varying.

Ultimately, we are going to have to broaden our paradigm of the subject. And if you are ready for that challenge, let's now further examine basic concepts of binding and loosing that Jesus taught His Jesus in context of prayer.

Back to Basics

As we look at the subject in context of prayer, it is important we know the literal definition of the words bind and loose. The word bind means to forbid, declare unlawful, or to disallow. The word loose means to allow, declare lawful, or to permit.

- Bind = disallow, declare unlawful, or forbid
- Loose = allow, declare lawful, or permit

Next, with the previous understanding in mind, let's look again into what the scripture really means when it speaks of binding and loosing in Matthew 16:19. The scripture is saying that if you allow, permit, or declare lawful what I have already allowed, permitted, and declared lawful in heaven, all of heaven will legally back you up. And if you disallow, forbid, or declare unlawful what I have already disallowed, forbidden, and declared unlawful in heaven, all of heaven will legally back you up.

We are literally called to enforce the laws of heaven in the earth through binding and loosing. However, I reiterate, there are prerequisites that must be considered in effectively doing so. We must first know what is legal and illegal in heaven, and the only way to do so is to know the word of God.

Proverbs teaches that when the King speaks, it becomes law. This means that everything God has promised acts as the divine protocol of everything that is either allowed or disallowed in the earth. What He has spoken has become legal, and it acts as constitutional rights that must be adhered to.

However, the laws of heaven are only enforced as we speak them. When we declare what the word of God says, it's like reciting Miranda rights prior to the enemy being placed under divine arrest.

If we ever embrace this revelation, it will change the game concerning what it means to engage in warfare prayer. Also, as we understand this truth, our binding and loosing would become more word-of-God conscious than it were devil-conscious in our practices of this type of prayer. Simply put, we cannot effectively bind and loose without understanding and referencing the appropriate supporting law, which in our case is the word of God.

137

Jonathan Ferguson

This is important, I reiterate, because many confuse
spiritual warfare with railing accusations, which actually
attract more demonic attacks than they actually conquer
(Jude 9-11). In fact, Jude 9 says in the Amplified that when
Michael contended with the devil, he judicially argued his
case. This means that our authority in prayer is not
measured by how ruthlessly we taunt at demons, but rather
how much of the word of God we can speak into the
atmosphere.

It is only as we utilize the word of God in prayer and
declarations that the enemy's activities are warranted as
illegal. And in addition, he is not only placed under divine
arrest, but vengeance is also executed upon him (Psalm
149:6-9).

This is yet another process that I will explain to you
in detail after I finish laying this foundation concerning
understanding the legalities of binding and loosing. I will
also show you what legalities have at all to do with battle,
but for now, just keep up with me.

The Legalities of Binding and Loosing

The words bind and loose are not magic words that
we use in prayer to make the devil behave, but they are
legal terms. In fact, in the Amplified version of Matthew
16:19, which is the closest to the original translation, it
literally depicts binding and loosing as that which is lawful
and unlawful. I couldn't reiterate enough that if we are
going to understand the power of binding and loosing, then
we must understand spiritual legalities.

Therefore, the intercession that takes place in
spiritual battle is very legal in nature. It consists of careful
mediation because if we position the case wrong, then we

can lose the battle. Effective warriors spend their time finding the right defense and using the proper negotiation strategies before God, our supreme judge, and even at times petitioning Him for angelic reinforcement in the battle.

Many do not see victory in warfare because they attempt to skip the legal negotiation process. However, we can become so powerful in intercession that the only hope for the devil himself is an attempt to negotiate our compromise over a legal settlement—just as he did with Jesus (Matthew 4:8-11).

When we bind and loose, we literally determine whether the enemy's activity in the earth will be penalized as against the law or not. In some cases we are the officers, in others the judge, in others the defense or prosecuting attorney, and in others the grand jury. We are not out to hunt demons, but rather praying and declaring the word of God in such a way that upholds the laws of heaven in the earth.

Examining Legalities & Praying Strategically

Considering the legalities of binding and loosing brings us full circle to once again focusing on praying strategically. We have previously learned that strategic prayer is not only praying the promises, but also praying the conditions of the promise. Now let's go deeper in that understanding as it pertains to binding and loosing, and in the meantime, be sure to review Chapter Three concerning how to pray strategically.

We must remember that to every promise in the word of God, there is a condition to that promise. In other words, there is something that God requires in the earth to bring the promise forth or give it permission to exist. Therefore, when God speaks, we must be careful to examine the conditions of His promise to determine if the criterion of the promise is being met so that it can come into manifestation.

Once we have prayed effectively in praying the promise, and prayed strategically in praying the conditions of the promise, there is yet another dimension. Warfare begins when and if we discern that there is yet another factor, particularly demonic in nature, causing the promise not to manifest. And once we get the revelation of any demonic activity influencing our surrounding conditions, we are then to learn how to apply the word of God specifically in those areas. Let me explain.

When we are aware of what legally belongs to us, we know the conditions are being met on our end, and yet there is still no manifestation, it is only at this point that we can properly discern if there is demonic activity that needs to be placed under divine arrest and dealt with for violating the laws of God. Paul described this as warring with the prophecy. This means that it is only as we accurately apply the word of God in specific areas of our lives through prayer and obedience that we can properly enforce spiritual laws in the earth.

Repentance is Key in Legalities and Battle Strategy

Just as our obedience is key in the promises of God being fulfilled, sin is also the key that opens up demonic doors and invites evil spirits in to hinder the fulfillment of the promise. Therefore, in warfare prayer, we will often find ourselves repenting for our sins as well as the sins of others, just as Daniel did in order for demonic doors to be closed.

Now I want to clarify something because there are many that say that we give the devil legal right, and I disagree. God is not democratic, so the devil will never have rights, but we often yield authority to the enemy when we sin.

There is no scripture that says the enemy has any legal right, but there are many scriptures that show how the enemy attempts to use laws and legalities against us (Daniel 7:25). Isaiah speaks of agreements and covenants with hell. In Romans 6, Paul mentions how obedience to sin can give sin the mastery over us. In Genesis, God informs Cain that sin was at the door and would come into him if he did not choose to do the right thing concerning his brother, Abel.

Good new is, no matter how the enemy works to find legal cause against us, our prayers of repentance break the contract and covenants. Repentance can bind the strongman and shut the door to the demonic. This is why the enemy uses temptations as peace negotiations (Matthew 4:1-11). He wants us to sin so that we compromise the legalities required in bringing him to justice.

Therefore, prayers of repentance are strategic acts of war, and we must be strategic in the way we pray prayers of repentance. In doing so, our repentance needs to often be both corporate and generational in nature, just as Daniel's prayers of repentance reflected. Let me explain.

At times, the demonic hindrances we encounter have nothing to do with any personal sin. However, in corporate repentance, we can ask God for forgiveness for the sins of the current generation we live in. And in generational repentance, we can ask God's forgiveness for the sins of the fathers, mothers, and ancestors before our times.

In both cases, we will find ourselves repenting for

sins that we have never committed so that we can in turn more effectively take authority over the demon that was invited in through the sin. When this happens, the enemy can no longer influence or determine the conditions surrounding the manifestation of the promise.

The Big Picture of Spiritual Warfare

You may be wondering why legalities have anything to do with warfare at all. If so, it's only because we have not been taught a big picture of the real battle that is taking place.

Most believe that binding and loosing is the totality of the battle, but I reiterate, it is not. In reality, the battle is waged on many different levels.

In order to understand the big picture of binding and loosing, we have to first understand that one of the main goals in warfare is to take over new territory and claim new land. When an army is successful in war, the land that it claims is then brought under the control and legal demands of the conquering government.

BUT ... there is always a remnant of people that remain under the laws of the former government. They are the ones who act as a resistance force to the new governmental regime.

For example, if China invaded America, they would most likely strategically target cities where they could most effectively dismantle its government, economics, and communications. The only problem would be that China would only be effective to the level that their militant strategy was strong enough to counter militant resistance from the cities remaining under American constitution.

A resistance force will often initiate political

uprisings and aggressive attacks designed for the opposing government's demise. And as long as there is a resistance team, reinforcement troops of the homeland's government can be sent into battle to regain control where it seemed that an enemy army had an advantage. Therefore, it doesn't matter how much ground that the enemy army has gained as long as the homeland government still stands.

Binding and Loosing: God's Resistance Force in the Earth

Although there have been demonic hierarchies set up throughout various territories according to Ephesians 6:12, the enemy knows that those who adhere to the laws of God's Kingdom are the resistance against his militant conquest. Therefore, God uses the revelation of binding and loosing to inform us that if we uphold the laws of our homeland, which is heaven, He will send in reinforcement troops into the battle to assist us in reclaiming territory. We are God's remnant resistance force in the earth.

When we bind and loose, we initiate a political uprising in the unseen world. We resist and we become the force that reclaims our God-given territories. God opens His armory to us, angelic reinforcement troops are dispatched to assist us in the resistance, and as we conquer, the enemy is legally penalized for war crimes.

This is why, according to Daniel 7:25, the enemy will ultimately seek to change the laws of the land he wants to conquest. It is what every invading army eventually has to do in order to maintain the victory. Truth is, the more individuals he can strip of their constitution, the more he can prevent a type of political uprising that can lead to his demise.

Therefore, I reiterate, legalities are a major issue

concerning the spiritual battles that are being waged. On one hand, God is empowering us to uphold His law and bring our enemy to justice. And on the other, we, as a resistance force, are not only upholding the law, but we are also deputized and armed to avenge in battle all violations against our constitution.

On the contrary, the enemy is tempting us to sin so that he can weaken the long-standing legalities that are forging the resistance against his intended conquest. He wants us to forsake our heavenly constitutional rights so that new laws forge the emergence of his demonic government. Too bad you are learning how to bind and loose.

Back to the Importance of Praying Strategically

Effective praying is very key because in binding and loosing, we must remember that the goal is to strategically target the root cause and core of the issue at hand, which requires strategic thinking. Truth is there are many layers of demonic activity that are to be examined in warfare and strategically dealt with. However, many enter the battle with mere zeal, rebuking devils, and they either have no idea of how to counteract their activity, or they enter the battle rebuking demons that are not the real demons that are in operation.

This is fallacy because the higher you go in warfare, the more strategic you must become. For example, it is not wise to launch a nuclear attack against a small fleet of soldiers, nor is it wise to shoot sniper bullets against stealth jets. In fact, in modern warfare, the higher you rank in authority, the farther you are from the battlefield.

As a war general, it would not be our job to attack every demon hiding behind every bush. We are to know enough about our enemy, our arsenal, our capabilities, and so forth in order to properly strategize the battle plan. Only then is the command given to either attack or to stand down.

I believe the scriptures speak of this wisdom in battle, specifically how wisdom is better than an armed man. It is not wise to enter warfare with a mere zeal to flex a spiritual muscle. Strategy is of the greatest essence because the battle is not won merely by the efforts of the soldiers on the battlegrounds, but by the generals who strategize the battle-moves behind the scene.

God, in this hour, is calling us back to the strategies that win the war, which are the very legalities and tactics that are deliberated behind the scenes of the battle at hand. This is what binding and loosing is about according to its foundational meaning. We are deliberating and examining the conditions of God's promises like attorneys at law who examine the evidence of a court case. We are then to determine guilty or not guilty, bound or loosed.

In strategic-level warfare prayer, we are primarily investigating the conditions surrounding the spiritual activity that takes place in the earth. We then enforce the law of heaven where there is illegal activity, and in doing so, there is vengeance and recompense executed on all violations. And believe it or not, at this point, we are ready to understand the very attack that can be executed on our spiritual enemies in spiritual warfare.

Chapter 15

Praying in Battle Mode

Chapter Objectives
- Understand the war tactic of opposition in binding and loosing.
- Understand the power that is released in prayer as we bind and loose.
- Understand how to deploy your spiritual weapons in prayer and more.

We are finally at the point in which you are ready to learn how to actually engage in an attack upon your spiritual enemies in prayer, should it become necessary. But first, let's begin to further examine more specifics concerning binding and loosing. You will now find that binding and loosing is the initial tactic in any lethal resolve we may engage in spiritual warfare prayer.

Therefore, I want to reiterate that binding and loosing are not "magic" words that make demons behave, neither are they merely religious rhetoric. But don't misunderstand me, there is nothing wrong with using the terminologies in prayer as long as there is an understanding of how to actually bind and loose effectively. However, ultimately, we do not bind and loose by merely saying "I bind" or "I loose."

More Foundation: How to Properly Bind and Loose

I don't think that I could reiterate enough that we bind and loose by strategically praying and decreeing the word of God. In fact, I want to also reiterate, according to Ephesians 3:10, that the way that we deal with demonic principalities and powers is not necessarily picking fights with them, but by making known to them the manifold wisdom of God. This means that our only job is to remind them of their defeat at Jesus's cross, and thereby establish the grounds of our authority.

Mark 11:22-24 teaches us that the reason prayer is powerful is because it activates the power of the spoken word. It also teaches us that we are to use our faith to not only pray, but also speak to mountains, which has a lot to do with prophesying and declaring the word of the Lord with authority. This means that what we ask of heaven we command in the earth because we have been given binding and loosing power.

The simple truth is that what we say will determine what is bound and what is loosed. This means that it doesn't matter how many demons we challenge in prayer if we are not saying anything of any significance. Therefore, we must embrace the fact that it is not coincidence that the only scripture in reference to how we deal with principalities and powers, other then wrestling with them, is found in Ephesians 3:10 and is in reference to declaring the wisdom of God.

The Power of Opposition

If we are going to truly understand how to effectively bind and loose, we must understand the power of opposition. Again, I recommend you purchase *Possessing the Gates of the Enemy* by Cindy Jacobs. She writes an awesome revelation about how to oppose the enemy that I want to briefly paraphrase.

Basically, in binding and loosing, so many focus so

much attention on the devil that they actually almost magnify him and thus empower him. Therefore, the power of opposition is a very strategic effort, and it is really simple to understand. Opposition is simply a resistance that we deploy that maneuvers the opposite of the enemy's onslaughts.

In other words, if the enemy is going left, we go right. If he is releasing hate, we release love. Sounds pretty simple, right? It is.

The simple truth is that in spiritual battle, in spite of what the enemy may be doing, we should be decreeing and declaring the word of God. Therefore, in order to effectively bind and loose, we must be more word-of-God conscious than we are devil conscious. We have to understand that for all demonic activity, there is a divine counter or opposite for it, and our words will determine what activity is legally reinforced in the heavens.

I reiterate, this is important because at times the way many engage in spiritual battle actuality attracts more warfare than it conquers. However, the key in walking out the victory is to understand that although we are aware of the demonic activity surrounding the battle, we do not give our energies and efforts to focusing on it. Now let me show you how this works.

For example, if we need dead things to be resurrected, we do not have to bind death if we call Lazarus forth (Selah). The truth is that if we prophesy to dead bones, which is a prophetic type of declaring the word, it will bind the spirit of death. It is a simple, yet profound reality.

Another great example is found in Mark 2 when Jesus did not address the man's paralysis therein, but He commanded him to walk. Instead of praying about the man's paralysis, Jesus spoke to the man's ability to walk in order to release his healing.

We too have to learn to command the solution instead of praying about the problem. We must remember that we are anointed to call those things that be not as though they were (Romans 4:17).

In binding and loosing, we have to make sure we are establishing the divine and not reinforcing the demonic with our words. I'm not saying that it is wrong to address the demonic, but if we are going to address the demonic, we must be sure we have both been clearly led by the Lord to do so, and that we have also established adequate word support.

If we will speak the word of God with authority, it will reinforce that word as law in the earth. And in most cases, this automatically binds the demonic assignment against the things that the word of God has promised for our lives.

This means that the authority we demonstrate in binding and loosing will be determined by how much of God's word we utilize in our prayer lives. Therefore, if we have not first learned how to strategically pray the promises of God and the conditions of those promises, we will likewise not be ready for strategic-level warfare prayer.

It does not matter how much we say we bind and loose if we are not validating it with the word of God. We have to fill our vocabulary with the word of God.

We have to provide legal grounds and reinforcement from the word of God concerning what we are saying in prayer. I couldn't emphasize enough that becoming more skillful in the way we pray and declaring the word of God remains key in all prayer—especially prayers pertaining to intercessory battle. (If this is a concept that is hard for you to grasp, it is probably because you either skipped over the last chapter, or you need to read it again.)

If we will decree and declare the word of God more in our attempts at binding and loosing, not only are we enforcing the law, but also there are many other things that we accomplish in the battle. The following list consists of the power in operation as we bind and loose.

An Overview of the Power in Operation When we Bind and Loose

1) Demons are Cast Down

Revelations 12 and Luke 10:17 are proof that demons can lose their high places. In fact, Luke 10 shows us that demons lose their place in the heavens as we accomplish what we are called to accomplish at ground level in the earth. We are not necessarily called to take on demonic principalities and powers directly and especially not individually, but simply rather to strategically decree, declare, and act on the word of God in the earth in ways that establish the grounds of our victory.

2) World Powers Shift

Notice how in Daniel 10:20, the spiritual battle shifted from being waged over Persia to being waged over Greece. This is significant in that the prayers of Daniel literally shifted the world power off of the nation of Persia.

When world powers shift, new eras begin to emerge, we dominate the air, and we create new culture. Successive and generational victories are released into our future. I recommend you purchase a book I wrote entitled *Prophets 101* and study the chapter on power shifts.

3) Demons are Disarmed

Colossians 2:15 is clear concerning how demonic principalities were disarmed and shamed with open mockery at the cross of Jesus. Therefore, every time we speak forth the things that are available to us in the word of God because of Jesus's death, burial, and resurrection, it is an act of disarming and shaming demonic principalities.

4) Demonic Powers are Crippled and Paralyzed

Psalm 8:2 teaches about a power that stills the avenger. It is powerful because the word *still* can literally mean to paralyze. It is also interesting to note that all of this is written in the context of the strength that God has ordained in our mouths. The simple truth is that we have power in our mouths when we pray to the very same extent that our praise can cripple and paralyze demonic forces.

Deploying the Weapons of our Warfare

It is only after we have effectively engaged in binding and loosing that our prayers actually go into an attack-mode in the spiritual battle that is being waged. And I reiterate, any attempt to progress into this stage of battle prior to the proper legalities, covering, and reinforcement have been established, will prove to be futile.

BUT ... when God grants and the stage has been properly set in the battle, we can actually do some real damage in the enemy's camp. However, I don't want you to understand this is mere theory.

I really want you to take hold of the following truths. And they are so effective that I am actually only going to take a brief moment to relay these truths to you because once you embrace them, you embrace a point of no return, and you instantly become a serious threat to hell in prayer.

2 Corinthians 10:4 tells us that the weapons of our warfare are mighty through God. The only problem is no one ever tells us what our weapons are.

Jeremiah 50:25 says that the Lord opens His arsenal of weapons and prepares them for the day of His anger. This means that we have an endless supply of weapons that we can utilize in the realm of the spirit, and I am going to attempt to explain how to release them in just a couple of sentences.

Hebrews 4 teaches us that the word of God is a weapon. And Ephesians 6 teaches us not only how the Word is a weapon, but also how prayer deploys the weapon. The revelation is that in the same way that prayer can deploy the sword of the Spirit; it also deploys all of the other weapons of our warfare.

The scriptures often mention various instruments of war utilized by God to annihilate demonic activity. At times, there were more familiar types of weapons such as arrows, spears, battle-axes, and more. However, at other times, there were weapons that were not so typical.

For example, even natural elements such as fire and wind were at times utilized as spiritual war technologies. And let's not forget the power of our praise, the name of Jesus, and the blood of Jesus. According to scripture they all have yielded devastating impact to the kingdom of darkness.

The good news is that, through prayer, we can literally open our mouths and deploy the same power by simply mentioning the blood of Jesus, the fire of God, the name of Jesus, or any other weapon that is made known to us by revelation of the word. This means that just as in a natural battle, we can cause the kingdom of darkness to experience war casualties.

Every time we open our mouth to speak forth the word of God, we ultimately strike a crippling blow upon our enemies. Literal pain and torment can be inflicted on the enemy when we deploy our spiritual weapons.

Scriptures speak on how the enemy can be vexed, smitten, put to fear, etc. (See warfare prayers of psalms in the prayer index). Therefore, when we pray, the enemy should be afraid that we would "push the red button" and unleash an all-out nuclear attack.

More study should be made in this area, but for now, the following is a very brief list of spiritual weapons that can be deployed in battle as we decree and declare the word of God. I'm only going to place scriptural references for the first two examples on the list, in order to give you an idea of what you should be looking for in the scriptures. Your homework is to search the word of God for the remaining scriptural references that can be utilized on the following list:

- The blood of Jesus – Revelations 12:11
- The name of Jesus – Philippians 2:10
- Arrows (hint: arrow of the Lord's deliverance) –
- Praise –
- Whirlwinds –
- The two-edged sword –
- The battle-axe –
- The fire of God –

Jonathan Ferguson

Remember:
The previous list consists of only a very few of the many
types of spiritual weaponry that the Lord has revealed to
me personally. As you fill in the appropriate scriptural
references, you will notice yourself developing a pattern of
being able to recognize other compatible examples
throughout the Bible that I have decided not to include.

Paying in Battle Mode

Praying in battle mode has a lot to do with the
mentality that you pray in because of the revelation you
have in prayer. This is key because in this realm of prayer,
you want to be sure you are applying a certain level of
intensity.

Ultimately, you understand that there are things you
pray and certain words you say that inflict literal torment
upon your spiritual foes. It may sound deep, but the
application of this is very practical. Let's utilize the
previous list to briefly examine.

For example, you may say, "I plea the blood of Jesus,"
and when you do, you realize that angels begin to overcome
the devil and his demons according to Revelations 12:11.
You may simply shout out the name of Jesus and realize
that every time you do so, demons are forced to their knees.

It's all about directing your words. And believe it or
not, deploying your spiritual weapons is just as easy. In fact,
I want to show you how.

If I wanted to utilize a particular weapon in spiritual
warfare, I would simply pick my weapon of choice and
direct my words to release that particular weapon. For
example, if I wanted to utilize the arrows of deliverance in
my prayer, I would simply open my mouth and say, "I

154

release the arrows of deliverance in Jesus name".

Pretty simple, right? Of course it is, but it is nothing short of powerful, especially when you apply these truths in great intensity.

Chapter 16

Secrets of War

Chapter Objectives:

- Learn how to manifest victories in battle without having to address the demonic.
- Review strategic prayers that wrestle down principalities and powers without attracting demonic retaliation.
- Understand the power of prayers that shift atmospheres and the importance of discerning spiritual climates and terrains in battle.
- Review truths that are important to remember as you advance in the battle.

Before I give the last instruction concerning this particular prayer focus we've been covering for the last couple of chapters, I want to be sure you've embraced a very important truth so far. You will find it to be key in shifting your paradigm in the art of war (especially if you may be feeling that this binding and loosing thing is just too complicated).

I want to remind you that there are strategic prayers that we can pray in the battle that will manifest the victory without us ever having to be directly active in binding and loosing, or even necessarily addressing the demonic realm directly. I have mentioned such prayers already throughout the teaching; however, I designed this section to recap on those significant truths.

Truth is, we can apply strategic methods in prayer that do not over emphasize the devil, do not attract backlash, and do not cause needless war casualties. In fact, in consideration of what we've learned of the demonic hierarchy, these are prayers that I believe should be prayed consistently in the midst of a spiritual battle as a type of cover-fire in prayer. Let me explain.

Cover-fire is a war tactic that basically allows one soldier to cover and watch another soldier's back that is assigned to more directly launch an assault. It is possible that many intercessors have experienced backlash because they were not properly covered in the battle that they engaged. Therefore, I reiterate, certain strategic battle prayers can cause us to conquer demonic principalities and powers without attacking presumptuously in ways that can end to our demise. These prayers are as follows:

1) Prayers of praise and worship
2) Praying in the Holy Ghost
3) Prayers that enforce the Lord's victory from the book of Psalms (See Prayer Index)
4) Prayers that strategically deal with principalities and powers (power in the air, seats of authority, opening of the gates)
5) Prayers that shift atmospheres

Out of all the previous, *prayers that shift atmospheres* are the only type of prayers that I have covered or at least referenced in the least detail. Therefore, I want to take a brief moment to examine.

Prayers that Shift Atmospheres

In ancient times, war generals were very selective in determining whether their armies would fight on mountains, hills, in deserts, or in valleys. They would pick certain terrains that would ensure them an advantage. If we convert this knowledge in spiritual warfare language, knowing the terrains would have a lot to do with spiritually discerning the atmosphere and knowing the conditions surrounding the warfare.

In fact, the mentioning of mountains, valleys, and hills in scripture was often descriptive of the spiritually climatic conditions that surrounded various spiritual territories. And if the conditions were hostile, there was an anointing, like that which rested on John the Baptist, to prepare a way in the wilderness (Matthew 3:3; Isaiah 40:3-5).

This means that hills can be brought low, valleys can be exalted, crooked places made straight, and rough places made smooth. In other words, there are prayers that have the power to shift atmospheres.

In spiritual battle you have to understand the significance of dealing with atmospheric terrains, and in doing so, you are bringing the battle to your grounds. If you learn how to discern and shift difficult atmospheres, you can, in many cases, begin to engage the battle on your terms as opposed to being a victim of demonic onslaughts. You are then able to properly position yourself in the battle and know what precautions to take in hostile environments.

Ancient warriors understood that the terrains they chose in battle would either result in their safety or would be to their demise. However, many who engage in spiritual battle do not realize that they often do so to their demise. Many enter attempting to attack demons that have combative advantages due to the atmospheric conditions surrounding their prayer lives.

This revelation is, yet, another reason why our warfare has to evolve beyond the mere zeal of attacking demonic powers. In fact, a great place to start implementing a track record of lasting spiritual victories is to start learning to pray prayers that shift atmospheres instead of prayers that pick fights with demons and devils.

NOTE: Be sure to refer to the index for a list of the prayers that enforce victory, shift atmospheres, and strategically deal with principalities and powers.

Three Important Things to Remember when Binding and Loosing

Most òf the battles that we deal with can be overcome in only applying the previous methods. However, what if if we find ourselves in a place there is a need to engage in binding and loosing? If there is no way around the careful strategizing and deliberating of the legalities that surround the battle at hand... The following consists of very important things we should remember in the process:

1) Focus more on the Word and presence of the Lord than you do demons.

The following is a list of things that will help us remember key truths in effectively keeping the proper perspective in binding and loosing:

- Use decrees and declarations to establish grounds of authority (Ephesians 3:10).
- Continue to pray strategically using the word of God as legal grounds & weapons of war (2 Corinthians 10:4).
- Use the tactic of opposition and release the counterpart of various demonic activities. Remember that we are declaring the solution instead of praying the problem.
- Pray the prayers of agreement realizing that we are not called to go into warfare alone.

2.) Endure and persist: Proverbs 24:10

Just because we don't see results the first time doesn't mean it's not working. Sometimes it's a wrestle and not a TKO (total knock out) (Ephesians 6:12;Daniel 10:20).

- Don't get distracted or entangled again (2 Timothy 2:1-5).
- Don't cower to demonic retaliation.

3.) Fulfill Obedience & Learn how to be under authority: 2 Corinthians 10:6

In a battle, you have to be willing and ready to take orders. This means that although it is important you understand the concept of binding and loosing, you should more importantly understand the power of your obedience to God's chosen authorities.

The reality is that we would be far more effective in battle submitting to authority than we would in an attempt to bind demons. Therefore, if we are going to be effective warriors, we must master the order of the centurion, which is to both have authority and be under authority (Matthew 8:9-11).

Everyone in the army cannot be a commander, which is why humility and submission are necessary. In fact, I want to reiterate that the higher you rank in the battle determines how much strategic information that needs to be relayed to you concerning the battle.

In other words, you may feel like you will never fully understand these truths, but as long as you are submitted to authority and are quick to obey instructions, you are just as important in the battle as any of the great generals in the army of God.

Other Important Things to Remember When in the Battle

- As we progress, you must keep record of victory and take time to reward yourself while always remaining spiritually alert (gather the spoil) – Luke 11:20-22; 1Corinthians 9:7

- Take time to strengthen yourself (city) – Proverbs 25:28; Psalm 147:13-14; Isaiah 58:10-12

- Train someone else to fight (2 Tim 2:1-5).

As we go back into the battle and gain more ground, we should remember that we gain ground little by little (Deuteronomy 7:22). Therefore, we must be generational in our approach to spiritual battle. This means we must be willing to promote the next generation that will continue the work we have begun if we are going to see any lasting victories.

For example, lets consider the spiritual battle that Elijah encountered at mount Carmel. It was there that Elijah wrought a great victory in spiritual warfare as he called fire down out of heaven.

However, immediately afterward, Jezebel threatened his life, and when he fled to a cave in response to her threat, he couldn't understand why he had not yet seen complete victory. The answer was that his next phase of ministry was to anoint the next generation who would finish the work he had started.

I explain this concept in more detail in my book *Prophets 101.* I highly recommend you read it, but for now, we only need to understand that Elijah's cave experience does not mean that he was not effective in confronting Jezebel; it just means that God was ready to take him to the

161

next dimension.

And he was only going to go to that next dimension as he focused his attention on empowering the next generation of leadership to conquer this particular adversary. Likewise, if we are going to be the triumphant church that we are called to be, we can not be afraid of preparing the "next" generation and empowering them to advance the Kingdom of God further than we have.

For example, I'm sure there is a "next" revelation to even this book that someone will be anointed to write one day, and I welcome that understanding. Despite all of the information revealed in this book, there is yet more that can be revealed to make us more effective in spiritual battle.

I have penned the portion that God has given to me, and I am well aware that there is so much more that can help us become more effective in spiritual warfare. For now, this book will suffice as a great foundation in where God is taking us in our understanding of the art of spiritual warfare and prayer.

Chapter 17

Recover All

Chapter Objectives:
- Understand why strategic action must follow strategic warfare prayer.
- Understand our mandate to advance the kingdom and more.

After we have taken the necessary actions in the attack, the only thing left to do in the battle is to recover all. We are to claim the reward of our labor. And in order to do this, we have to understand that we are not in battle for spiritual exercise, but we are in this to claim some goods.

David was given this revelation in battle when he asked the Lord "shall I pursue". The Lord answered him and not only instructed him to pursue and overtake, but also to recover all (1 Samuel 30:8). The revelation is that the battle does not end at merely overtaking our enemy. After the enemy is dealt with, there is corresponding action remaining on our part. We must recover all.

Warfare is more than binding and loosing, decreeing and declaring. We must take action and claim territory. In other words, strategic warfare must always be enforced with strategic actions. The truth is that we only see maximum results as we become strategic in our thinking, our praying, and in our actions.

Jonathan Ferguson

Warring and Working

One of the greatest things we can do in battle is keep working. Nehemiah demonstrated this well as he instructed the workers, who were rebuilding the temple walls, to carry a weapon in one hand and a building tool in the other (Nehemiah 4:17-18). I want to reiterate that when Jesus gave the disciples power to tread down demonic forces; He was not merely telling them that the devil was under their feet.

We must remember that the word tread is a term used to describe a militant invasion. In other words, Jesus was telling them that their authority was in their forward movement. Power to tread means that we receive power to advance the kingdom, and as we do, demons lose ground in nations, cultures, and generations.

Claiming the Spoil

According to the scripture, we cannot bind the strongman until we enter into his house. This is key because many prayer warriors make the mistake of believing that everything there is to be done to the strongman is done in intercession. However, at some point, we have to actually enter into the arena where the strongman is active if we are going to overthrow his activity.

Furthermore, after the strongman is bound, and his stronghold is taken, the only thing left to do is to confiscate his goods and prized possessions. This means that every resource the enemy used to wage war and advance his kingdom now becomes the resources that accommodate our mission, purpose, and divine assignment.

We must move forward in our areas of assignment

utilizing all means necessary to promote the gospel of the kingdom. We must be willing to act and move into the arenas in which the enemy once had control. And in order to do that, we must talk Babylon while we think Kingdom, which means we must be relevant to the world in our faith approach. I couldn't reiterate enough how it takes strategic battle and strategic actions for manifested victory.

Advancing the Kingdom

Ultimately, if our spiritual warfare does not eventually become about and result in the kingdom of God being advanced, we have missed the point. If the gospel is not being preached with power and demonstration, we have missed the point.

If souls are not being saved and discipled, and if believers are not being trained to occupy their God-given spheres of society in order to effect change and cause reformations in culture and generations, it is then evident, no matter how much spiritual warfare we think we are doing, that our victory, yet, remains unclaimed. If you are serious about this, I STRONGLY recommend you read my book *Jesus in HD (High Demand): Prophetic Insight into Revival & Evangelism.*

It is our responsibility to take action and advance in the sphere assigned to us, whether it is business, the arts, ministry, or etc. And if we do not strategize our forward movement, it will ultimately prove that we are really not interested in praying effectively as we should be. It will be proof that for some reason we get some type of weird satisfaction in making a lot of noise and calling it prayer.

Jonathan Ferguson

Occupy

I want to reiterate that we must be willing to occupy the spheres that were once occupied by demonic forces. This means that the warfare extends beyond being able to war in the Spirit through prayer.

After we master the prayer portion, there is yet more work to be done. The purpose of this book is not necessarily to elaborate on such, but I can give you some tips on what will help us recover all as we move forward into various arenas.

Simply put, we must have the necessary balance of ability and visibility as we move forward in our prospective spheres advancing the Kingdom of God. And we must understand the two so that we can properly balance the two. Lets take a moment to review the following key factors that will aid us in advancing the Kingdom in our current culture.

Merging Ability and Visibility

A) We need ability

I once heard someone say that great publicity only causes a bad product to fail faster. If we are going to move forward, we should be cultivating our gifting and God-given talents. We should be sharpening our anointing and preparing ourselves for our destinies. We must have a healthy ambition to be second to none when it comes to what we do best and what God has called us to do.

Lastly, we should remember that our ability is by far not limited to gifts and talents. We have power to raise the dead, heal the sick, and evict the demons that plague the quality of our social economy. No one else can offer this to the world.

What is inside of us is literally put on demand. And because of this the church can be positioned in ways that impact our culture in ways that cause demonic activity to lose its relevance. This leads to the importance of visibility.

B) We need visibility

Once our gifting is cultivated and ready for the world, we then need visibility. And in order to take advantage of our current culture's platform, our branding must become professional and cutting edge in graphics. We must become innovative in the way we represent ourselves and utilize mass communications: publishing, media, radio, apps, and other tools. These are the things that affect culture as we have previously learned.

As warriors we must understand that media exposure will be one of the major keys in regaining ground and recovering all. Therefore, the way we support the concept of media ministry in prayer will play a key role in how we effectively wage spiritual battle and manifest the victory. We must understand that it does not matter how much ability and power we have to impact our world if we do not have visibility.

There is a lot we can learn from Moses, who defeated many demonically possessed kings, in how he acknowledged the anointing on his life to publish the name of the Lord (Deuteronomy 32:3). Likewise, we should embrace this responsibility to publish over the airways via media and mass communications (Psalm 19:1-4). And as prayer warriors, we should be praying that the necessary resources are supplied that allow for media ministry to be done in the spirit of excellence.

This is what being strategic in battle is all about. It makes no difference how much binding and loosing we enjoy engaging in if we are not going to take the time and understand the battle and appropriately respond in ways that outwit our adversary. I'm sure there is a lot covered in this chapter that stretched your paradigm of what spiritual warfare is all about, and that is exactly what my goal is.

We have to get to the place where we understand that this spiritual battle extends far beyond prayer and yet must never be engaged apart from it. And as we do, we need strategy because wisdom is better than the mighty man.

It's time that we cease to continue engaging in worthless and meaningless religious activities in the name of spiritual warfare. If we are going to fight this fight of faith, lets do it effectively.

I pray you will refuse to be a novice in your approach to the battle that is waging in the spirit, from this day forward. I pray that this book has provoked you to understand the battle and how to properly engage it. And I pray you take the time to review this material over and over again until you embrace the mind of a true warrior and become skilled in the art of spiritual warfare prayer.

Well ... this is as far as we go in examining this concept. However, I reiterate that the perfect follow up to this book is my book *Jesus in HD (High Demand): Prophetic Insight into Revival & Evangelism*. I only wanted to take this chapter to initially introduce you to the reality that it is only as we advance the Kingdom of God in the earth that we claim the spoils of warfare prayer.

Now in conclusion of this book, I want to take the next chapter and briefly give you some principles that will help you as you apply the truths that you have learned pertaining to prayer. If you are serious about being in this for the long run, this final word is going to give you the necessary tools in your pursuit of establishing a powerful prayer life.

Chapter 18

How to Implement a Successful Track Record in Prayer

Chapter Objectives:
- Understand the three primary ways that answers come to prayer.
- Review how to discern when the answer is released in prayer.
- Review more on how to overcome feelings of apathy, dryness, and resistance in prayer and more.

One of the most important factors in seeing more results in prayer is to develop an ability to discern the release of God's response to your prayer. Many pray and God answers them; however, they are discouraged because they do not discern the manner in which God releases the answer.

For example, Israel prayed in Egypt that God would deliver them from bondage, but when God answered them, it was not in Egypt; it was in Midian. The children of Israel were praying in Egypt, yet God sent the answer to their prayers to Midian (Exodus 4:19).

The truth is that it is possible to pray from one place and for God to answer from another. Don't misunderstand me because I'm speaking spiritually here.

In other words, we can be praying and expecting God to answer our prayers in one way, yet, in reality He answers in another. Therefore, if we are going to properly discern the spiritual release to our prayers, we have to begin with understanding the three primary ways that answers come to our prayer as follows:

- Revelation
- Transformation
- Manifestation

Transformation is when prayer changes us. Revelation is when God either reveals Himself or gives us the instruction needed in order to see the manifestation of what we are praying. Lastly, manifestation is when what we are praying for actually materializes. And even in manifestation, a process is often required.

This is why learning to discern the spiritual release in prayer is important. For example, sometimes we are looking for manifestation when God is releasing revelation, which requires a process of instruction, obedience, and an adjustment of maybe even our prayer focus at times.

If there is a process connected to the manifestation, we have to be willing to acknowledge the gradual results in prayer in order to keep up with the process and not abort it. It is like spiritually tracking our miracle by constantly evaluating our prayer lives and building on the successes gradually.

That's right, your miracle has a tracking number. I won't even attempt to elaborate. I'd rather just let you think about that for a moment.

Celebrating the Presence of Jesus

Instead of getting discouraged with the lack of results we believe we are experiencing, we should give more attention to and place more value on the tangible presence of God that comes in prayer. Only times in His presence can create breakthrough atmospheres and manifestations even beyond what you believe for.

It is in an atmosphere of His presence that the revelation and instruction comes that leads us into the manifestation of what we are praying for. We have to learn to cooperate with this reality, and we only do so with experience.

Sometimes the tangible presence of God will completely change the manner in which we are praying. At other times, the revelation that comes in that atmosphere will change our perspective about what we are praying.

There are also times when the atmosphere in prayer will provoke us in embracing global prayer concerns. We should embrace the shifting in realization that as we pray God's concerns, He will take care of ours.

There are so many different shifts we learn to cooperate with as we pray Spirit-led prayers. It is up to us to learn through experience the nature of how our prayers are answered so that we don't sabotage or forfeit the release. As you continue to fully grasp this concept, I recommend that you refer to the chapter entitled *Prayers that Break into the Supernatural* and review the teaching therein.

Never Quit Engaging in Prayer

The best way to build a track record and consistency is to never quit engaging in prayer. There is a solution to getting past the dryness in prayer. There is a solution to the feelings that maybe your prayers are not accomplishing anything.

Truth is, some days just don't seem as anointed in prayer, especially when you are trying to break into higher realms in God. You must however remain desperate to lay hold of God in a supernatural way and continue to press in. You can review the following and apply the principles in order to experience personal breakthrough in your prayer life:

- Apply principles of increasing intensity in prayer (Review Chapter 5).

- Stir up yourself by remembrance: It is possible to reconnect to a place of anointing by simply remembering it. Meditating on the reality of a past encounter with the Lord in prayer can become a doorway back into an encounter (Review Chapter 3).

- Allow the Holy Ghost to groan through you (Romans 8:26-27).

- Press past emotions and feelings: Our feelings and emotions represent the outer courts of prayer, which are lower realms in the spirit. There is a deeper place in the holy of holies, and the only way to get there is to disregard the feelings that we have when our flesh and our emotions do not want to go there. In fact, heaviness, tiredness, or weariness often come prior to a breakthrough in prayer.

We must not allow ourselves to quit due to feelings of not accomplishing anything in prayer. We must remember that prayer always works in our favor. The book of Proverbs teaches that in all labor, there is profit. That means it is impossible to seriously work at something and not eventually experience some rewarding results. Again, we must press past how and what we feel and become desperate to encounter our God.

For this is what prayer is all about. It is to know what it is to live in a God encounter—to know Him, to walk with Him, and to be like Him. It is beyond ecstasy and a

Jonathan Ferguson

reality that you only experience when you finally realize
that it is worth fighting for.

Chapter 19

Index of Prayers

Chapter Objectives:
- Worship Warrior Prayers
- Prayers for God to fight our battles
- Prayers that expose and reverse the strategies of the enemy
- Prayers that vex demons
- Prayers that shift atmospheres and more

Prayer Devotionals #1:

Worship Warrior Prayers- Jesus Our Man of War

I want to begin this chapter with prayers of worship and praise. Remember that we were taught by Jesus to hallow His name first as we enter into a place of prayer (Matthew 6:10).

Jesus You Are:

- Alpha & Omega (Revelations 1:8)
- Beginning & Ending (Revelations 1:8)
- 1st & Last + from age to age you remain the same (Revelations 1:11)
- You change not (Malachi 3:6)
- The same yesterday, today, and forever (Hebrews 13:8)
- Which is, and was, and is to come-the almighty (Revelations 1:8)
- The ancient of days (Daniel 7:9)
- Author & finisher of our faith (Hebrews 12:2)
- Rock of our salvation (Psalm 89:26)

- The yes + the amen (Revelations 3:14)
- The resurrection & life (John 11:25)
- Lamb of God (John 1:29)
- Lion of Judah (Revelations 5:5)
- Root of David + offspring of Jesse (Revelations 5:5)
- Seed of Abraham (Galatians 3:16)
- Desire of the nations (Haggai 2:7)
- Faithful and true witness + beginning of the creation of God (Revelations 3:14)
- The life of man-light of life (John 1:4)
- Bread of life (John 6:48)
- True vine (John 15:1)
- Lily of the valley + rose of Sharon (Song of Solomon 2:1)
- The chief shepherd (John 10:11; 1 Peter 5:4)
- Bishop of our soul (1 Peter 2:25)
- Our advocate with the father (1 John 2:1)
- The propitiation for our sins (1 John 2:2)
- Apostle + high priest of our profession (Hebrews 3:1)
- Mediator of the better covenant (Hebrews 8:6)
- The day spring from on high (Luke 1:78)
- Emanuel: God with us (Matthew 1:23)
- Son of the living God (Matthew 16:16)
- Wonderful, counselor, mighty God, everlasting Father, prince of peace (Isaiah 9:6)

You Are Our:

- Shelter (Psalm 61:3)
- Fortress (Psalm 71:3; 91:2; 144:1-2)
- Refuge (Psalm 14:6; 91:2)
- Dwelling place (Psalm 90:1)
- Secret place + hiding place + resting place (Psalm 91:1)
- Strong tower + high tower (Psalm 61:3; 144:1-2)
- Rock (Psalm 62:2; 71:3)

- Strength-of my heart (Psalm 27:7; 118:14; 114:1-2)
- Pavilion (Psalm 27:5)
- Firm foundation (Psalm 73:26; 119:57)
- Shield/sword (Psalm 27:7; 84:11; 91:4; 144:1-2)
- Defense (Psalm 62:2; 89:18)
- Buckler (Psalm 91:4)
- Safety/cover (Proverbs 21:32)
- Helper (Psalm 54:4)
- Deliverer (Psalm 114:1-2)
- Salvation (Psalm 118:14)
- King + judge + ruler + portion (Psalm 73:26; 119:57)
- Goodness (Psalm 114:1-2)
- Song [satisfaction, delight, pleasure, fulfillment] (Psalm 118:14)
- Exceeding great reward (Genesis 15:1)

King of Kings:

- King of kings (1 Timothy 6:15).
- Lord of lords (Revelations 17:14).
- Governor & king among the nations (Psalm 22:28; Jeremiah 10:7).
- Government is on your shoulder (Isaiah 9:6).
- Increase of government never ends (Isaiah 9:7).
- Live forever + dominion is everlasting (Daniel 4:34).
- Kingdom shall not be destroyed (Daniel 7:14).
- Kingdom from generation to generation (Daniel 4:34).
- Dominion shall not pass away (Daniel 7:14).
- You sit upon your throne & kingdom to order it & establish it with judgment/justice (Isaiah 9:7).
- King of glory + strong & mighty (Psalm 24:8-9).
- Mighty in battle (Psalm 24:8-9).
- The Lord our mighty warrior (Isaiah 42:13).
- You go before us & fight our battle (Deuteronomy 1:30).

- Lord of hosts (Psalm 24:10).
- Captain of hosts (Joshua 5:15).
- God of the angelic armies + Ruler of the armies of heaven (Daniel 4:35).
- Jehovah Saboath – Master Avenger (James 5:4)
- Man of war (Exodus 15:3).
- Chiefest among 10,000 [General, commanding officer] (Song of Solomon 5:10).
- The day of vengeance in your heart + year of your redeemed (Isaiah 63:4).
- You will travel in the greatness of His strength + speak as 1 mighty to save (Isaiah 63:1).
- Your voice shall beat down armies that rise against, and you shall beat down enemies (Isaiah 30:31).
- You tread them in your anger + trample them in your fury (Isaiah 63:3).
- You put on righteousness as breastplate, salvation as helmet (Isaiah 59:17).
- You put on vengeance as clothing and zeal as cloak (Isaiah 59:17).
- Your garments stained with the blood of our enemies (Isaiah 63:3).
- In battles of shaking, you will fight for us (Isaiah 30:32).
- Your own arm shall bring salvation (Isaiah 59:16, 19; Isaiah 63:5).
- Your own righteousness shall sustain you (Isaiah 59:16, 19; Isaiah 63:5).
- When the enemy comes in like a flood, you lift a standard (Isaiah 63:5).
- When enemies come one way, you smite them before our face and they flee seven ways (Deuteronomy 28:7).
- You are the Christ, Messiah, anointed King (Matthew 16:16).
- You are anointed to destroy the yoke + remove the burden –the yoke destroyer + burden

remover (Isaiah 10:27).

- Your yoke is easy + burden light (Matthew 13:30).
- You break the yoke of our burden (Isaiah 9:4).
- You break the staff off our shoulder (Isaiah 9:4).
- You break the rod of our oppressor (Isaiah 9:4).
- You're anointed to preach gospel (Isaiah 61:1-3).
- You're anointed heal the broken + release captive + open prison (Isaiah 61:1-3).
- You're anointed to change the season (Luke 4:18).
- You are the Lord of the release; God of the acceptable year/time + year of Lord's release (Luke 4:18).
- You're anointed to proclaim the acceptable year + the due season + the kairos moment (Luke 4:18).
- The appointed time + the "now" anointing (Luke 4:18).
- You ordain the suddenly & perform the immediately (Luke 4:18).
- You're anointed to release from debt and poverty + avenge the enemy (Isaiah 61:1-3).
- You comfort those that mourn + appoint beauty for ashes (Isaiah 61:1-3).
- You appoint oil of joy for mourning + appoint garments of praise (Isaiah 61:1-3).
- You appoint double for shame (Isaiah 61:1-3).

- Jehovah Nissi = the Lord our victory & banner (Exodus 17:15).
- None can stop/stay your hand (Daniel 4:35).
- You always cause us to triumph and give us the victory (2 Corinthians 2:14; 1 Corinthians 15:57-58).
- You teach our hands to war + arms to battle + fingers to fight (Psalm 18:34).
- Great deliverance you give to your king and your anointed (Psalm 18:50).

179

Prayer Devotionals #2:

Warfare Prayers from the books of Psalms- Prayers that petition God for the victory

Prayers that Expose & Reverse the Strategies of the Enemy:

- Destroy them + let them fall by their own counsel + cast them out (Psalm 5:10).
- Let them return and be ashamed suddenly (Psalm 6:10).
- Cause them to fall into the pit and ditch they have dug and made (Psalm 7:15).
- Let their mischief return upon their own heads (Psalm 7:16).
- Let their violent dealing come down on their own plate (Psalm 7:16).
- Let my enemies be turned back (Psalm 9:3).
- Rebuke the heathen + destroy the wicked (Psalm 9:5).
- Make their destructions come to a perpetual end (Psalm 9:6).
- Let them be taken in their own devices that they have imagined (Psalm 10:2).
- Help us find out our enemies and those that hate us (Psalm 21:8).
- Make them where they are not able to perform the intended evil + imagined mischievous devices (Psalm 21:11).
- Make them turn back in battle + make ready arrows against their faces (Psalm 21:12).
- Break the bow + cut the spear asunder + burn the chariot in fire (Psalm 46:9).

- When they bend their bow & shoot arrows, let them be cut in pieces (Psalm 58:7).

- Hide us from the secret counsel & insurrection of the enemy (Psalm 64:2).
- Make their own tongue fall upon themselves (Psalm 64:8).
- Rebuke until they submit themselves with pieces of silver (Psalm 68:30).
- Make them pay tolls & be fined for trespassing our territory & possession (Psalm 68:30).
- Let their table become a snare before them (Psalm 69:22).
- That which should have been for their welfare let it become a trap (Psalm 69:22).
- Render seven fold their reproach into their own bosom (Psalm 79:12).
- Let them cover themselves with their own confusion as with a mantle (Psalm 109:29).
- Make us wiser than our enemies that are ever with us (Psalm 119:98).
- As for the head of them that compass us about, let the mischief of their own lips cover them (Psalm 140:9).
- Deliver us from evil men + preserve us from the violent man who hath purposes to overthrow our goings (Psalm 140:1,4).
- Keep us from the snares and gins of workers of iniquity (Psalm 141:9).
- Let the wicked fall into their own nets while I escape (Psalm 141:10).
- We decree that the snare is broken and we are escaped (Psalm 124:7).

Prayers that Vex Demons:

- Laugh from the heavens (Psalm 2:4).
- Have them in derision (Psalm 2:4).
- Speak to them in your wrath (Psalm 2:5).
- Vex them in your sore displeasure (Psalm 2:5).
- Let all my enemies be ashamed + sore vexed (Psalm 6:10).
- Let them return from where they came + be shamed suddenly (Psalm 6:10).
- Arise + disappoint our enemies + cast them down (Psalm 17:13).
- Let their eyes be darkened that they cannot see (Psalm 69:23).
- Let their loins continually shake for fear (Psalm 69:23).
- Let them be confounded & consumed that are enemies to our soul (Psalm 71:13).
- Let them be covered with reproach & dishonor that seek our hurt (Psalm 71:18).
- Let them be confounded & brought to shame that seek our hurt (Psalm 71:24).
- Put them to a perpetual reproach (Psalm 78:66).
- Persecute them with thy tempest (Psalm 83:15).
- Make them afraid with thy storm (Psalm 83:15).
- Take them away in thy whirlwind (Psalm 58:9).
- Fill their faces with shame (Psalm 83:16).
- Let them be confounded & troubled forever (Psalm 83:17).
- Let them be put to shame & perish that men may know that thou whose name alone is Jehovah art most high over all the earth (Psalm 83:17-18).
- Show me a token for good that they, which hate us, may see it and be ashamed (Psalm 86:17).
- Plague them that hate us (Psalm 89:22).
- Let my adversaries be clothed with shame (Psalm 109:29).
- Let the wicked see and be grieved + Nash with teeth + melt away (Psalm 112:10).

- Clothe our enemies with shame & let our crowns flourish (Psalm 132:18).

Basic Petitions & Declarations for Warfare:

- Give the heathen as our inheritance (Psalm 2:8).
- I will not be afraid of 10,000s that have risen themselves against us (Psalm 3:6).
- Arise and save (Psalm 3:7).
- Arise in your anger (Psalm 7:6).
- Lift up thyself because of the rage of our enemies (Psalm 7:6).
- Awake for us to the judgment that thou hast commanded (Psalm 7:6).
- Prepare thy throne to judgment (Psalm 9:7).
- Have mercy + consider the trouble & suffering of them that hate us (Psalm 9:13).
- Lift us up from the gates of death (Psalm 9:13).
- Lighten our eyes lest we sleep the sleep of death (Psalm 13:3).
- Hear in the day of trouble, help, defend, & strengthen out of Zion (Psalm 20:1-2).
- Save your anointed with the saving strength of your right hand (Psalm 20:6).
- Thou art our God from our mother's womb (Psalm 22:10).
- Be not far, our strength, make haste to help us (Psalm 22:19).
- Deliver our soul from the sword + our darling from the power of the dog (Psalm 22:20).
- Save us from the lion's mouth, for thou hast heard us...(Psalm 22:21).
- Let thy rod & staff comfort us that we fear no evil (Psalm 23:4).
- Even in the presence of our enemies, prepare a table (Psalm 23:5).

- Lift up your heads gates/doors, and the king of Glory shall come in (Psalm 24:7-9).
- I trust in thee, let us not be put to shame (Psalm 25:2).
- Don't let our enemies triumph over us (Psalm 25:2).
- Let none that wait on thee be ashamed (Psalm 25:3).
- The Lord is our light & salvation of whom shall we fear or be afraid (Psalm 27:1).
- When the wicked, my enemies & foes come upon us to eat our flesh they stumbled and fell (Psalm 27:2).
- Though a host should encamp against us, our heart shall not fear (Psalm 27:3).
- Though war should arise against us, in this will we be confident "one thing" (Psalm 27:3-4).
- In the time of trouble, He shall hide us in His pavilion, in the secret of His tabernacle, and set us upon a rock (Psalm 27:5).
- Now shall our heads be lifted up above our enemies (Psalm 27:6).
- Thou art our king; command deliverance for Jacob (Psalm 44:4).
- Through you, we will push down our enemies (Psalm 44:5).
- Through thy name, we will tread down our enemies (Psalm 44:5).
- I will not trust in my bow neither my sword to save us (Psalm 44:6).
- Thou hast saved us from our enemies + put to shame them that hated us (Psalm 44:7).
- You make wars to cease (Psalm 46:9).
- Be exalted among the heathen + the Lord of host is with us (Psalm 46:10-11).
- Subdue the people under + the nations under our feet (Psalm 47:3).
- God is gone up with a shout + the Lord with the sound of the trumpet (Psalm 47:5).
- Deliver us out of all trouble + let our eyes see our

desire upon our enemies (Psalm 54:7).

- Give us help in trouble; vain is the help of man (Psalm 60:11).
- Through God, we shall do valiantly (Psalm 60:12).
- You are our rock, salvation, defense + we shall not be greatly moved (Psalm 62:2).
- Those who imagine mischief shall be slain (Psalm 62:3).
- Although they consult to cast you down from your excellency, they delight in lies, and they bless with the mouth/curse inwardly yet WE SHALL NOT BE MOVED (Psalm 62:4-5).
- Preserve our lives from fear of the enemy (Psalm 64:1).
- Don't let the rebellious exalt themselves (Psalm 66:7).
- Strengthen that which thou have wrought from us (Psalm 68:28).
- Don't hide thy face from thy servant; when in trouble hear us speedily (Psalm 69:17).
- Draw nigh to our soul to redeem it (Psalm 69:18).
- Deliver us because of our enemies (Psalm 69:18, 19-21).
- Forsake us not until we have shown thy strength to this generation (Psalm 71:18).
- Your enemies shall fear as long as the sun and moon endure throughout all generations (Psalm 72:5).

Prayers for God to Fight the Battle:

- Break our enemies a rod of iron (Psalm 2:9).
- (Thou hast smitten) smite all mine enemies upon the cheekbone (Psalm 3:7).

- (Thou hast broken) break the teeth of the ungodly (Psalm 3:7).

185

- Let praise still the avenger (Psalm 8:2).
- Turn not, whet your sword, bend your bow & make it ready (Psalm 7:12).
- Prepare the instruments of war (Psalm 7:13).
- Ordain your arrows against the persecutors (Psalm 7:13).
- Let them fall and perish at thy presence (Psalm 9:3).
- Bring them down to fall, cause us to rise and stand upright (Psalm 20:18).
- Swallow them in your wrath + let fire devour them (Psalm 21:9).
- Destroy their fruit from the earth + their seed from the children of men (Psalm 21:10).
- Destroy violence and strife in the city + divide their tongues (Psalm 55:9).
- Bring them down into the pit of destruction (Psalms 55:23).
- Let the bloody & deceitful not live out half their days because I trust in you (Psalm 55:23).
- (Shall they escape in iniquity?) Cast them down in your anger (Psalm 56:7).
- Break their teeth in their mouth (Psalm 58:6).
- Break out the teeth of the young lions (Psalm 58:6).
- Break the arm of the wicked (Psalm 37:17).
- Let them melt away as the waters that run continually (Psalm 58:7).
- Let everyone of them pass away like an untimely birth that they may not see the sun (Psalm 58:8).
- Tread down our enemies (Psalm 60:12).
- Make them as the bowing wall + tottering fence (Psalm 62:3).
- Shoot at them with arrows + wound them suddenly (Psalm 64:7).
- Scatter them that delight in war (Psalm 68:30).
- Break in pieces the oppressor (Psalm 72:4).
- Break the heads of the dragons in waters (Psalm 74:13).

- Break the head of leviathan in pieces (Psalm 74:14).
- Smite our enemies in their hinder parts (Psalm 78:66).

- Cause the haters of the Lord to submit themselves (Psalm 81:15).
- Subdue our enemies + turn your hand against our adversaries (Psalm 81:14).
- Let them become as the dung of the earth (Psalm 83:10).
- Make them like a wheel as stumble before the wind (Psalm 83:13).
- As fire burns wood & as the flame that sets the mountains on fire (Psalm 83:14).
- Make your enemies your footstool (Psalm 110:1).
- Send the rod of thy strength out of Zion + rule in midst on your enemies (Psalm 110:2).
- Cut asunder the cords of the wicked (Psalm 129:4).
- Stretch forward thy hand against the wrath of our enemies (Psalm 138:7).
- Let burning coals fall upon them (Psalm 140:10).
- Cast them into fire + into deep pits that they rise up not again (Psalm 140:10).
- Let no evil speaker be established in the earth (Psalm 140:11).
- Let evil hunt the violent to overthrow him (Psalm 140:11).
- Of thy mercy cut off our enemies (Psalm 143:12).
- Destroy all that afflict our soul...for I am thy servant (Psalm 143:12).
- Cast the wicked down to the ground (Psalm 147:6).

More Basic Warfare Prayers and Declarations:

- You shall have dominion from sea to sea + from the rivers to the ends of the earth (Psalm 72:8).

- They that dwell in the wilderness shall bow before you (Psalm 72:9).
- Your enemies shall lick the dust (Psalm 72:9).
- All kings fall before you + all nations serve you (Psalm 72:11).
- Redeem our souls from deceit & violence; precious our blood is in your sight (Psalm 72:14).
- (There are no signs/no prophet)+ how long shall our adversary reproach? (Psalm 74:9-11).
- Shall the enemy blaspheme forever? Withdraw your hand + pluck it out of thy bosom (Psalm 74:9-11).
- You are the king of the earth working salvation in the midst of the earth (Psalm 74:12).
- Divide the sea by thy strength (Psalm 74:13).
- Remember this that the enemy hath reproached oh Lord + foolish people have blasphemed thy name (Psalm 74:18).
- Deliver not the soul of thy turtledove to the multitude of the wicked (Psalm 74:19).
- Forget not the congregation of the poor + have respect to thy covenant (Psalm 74:19-20).
- Arise +plead your own cause + remember how foolish men reproach daily (Psalm 74:22).
- Forget not the voice of your enemies, the tumult of them that rise up against thee increase continually (Psalm 74:23).
- All the horns of the wicked are also cut off but the horns of the righteous shall be exalted (Psalm 75:10).
- God is known in Judah + in Salem is His tabernacle +dwelling place is Zion (Psalm 76:1-2).
- There He breaks the arrows of the bow, the shield, and the battle (Psalm 76:3).
- At thy rebuke (God of Jacob), both chariot & horse are cast into deep sleep (Psalm 76:6).
- Cast off the spirit of the princes + be terrible to the kings of the earth (Psalm 76:12).

- You declared thy strength among the people + with your arm redeemed them (Psalm 77:14-15).

- The waters saw & were afraid + the depths were troubled (Psalm 77:16).
- The skies sent out a sound + arrows went out abroad (Psalm 77:17).
- Voice of thy thunder in heaven = lightening lightened the world + earth feared and was still (Psalm 77:18).
- Awake as one from sleep + like a mighty man that shouts by reason of wine (Psalm 78:66).
- Help us for the glory of thy name + deliver & purge away our sin (Psalm 79:9).
- Wherefore should the heathen say, where is our God? (Psalm 79:10).
- Be known among the heathen in our sight by the revenging of the blood of thy servants (Psalm 79:10).
- According to the greatness of thy power preserve those appointed to die (Psalm 79:11).
- Cause our adversaries to perish at the rebuke of thy countenance (Psalm 80:16).
- Redeem and deliver our soul from the lowest hell (Psalm 86:13).
- Establish your arm with us + let your arm strengthen us (Psalm 89:21).
- And the enemy shall not exact upon us nor the son of wickedness afflict us (Psalm 89:22).
- Beat down our foes before our face; plague them that hate us (Psalm 89:23).
- My eye shall see my desire upon my enemies + my ear shall hear my desire of the wicked that rise up against me (Psalm 92:11).
- Loose those appointed to death (Psalm 102:20).
- Bring out of darkness & the shadow of death + break our bands asunder (Psalm 107:14).

- Break the gates of brass + cut the bars of iron in pieces (Psalm 107:16).
- Through God we shall do valiantly + He shall tread down our enemies (Psalm 108:13).
- The heavens are the Lords and the earth belongs to the children of men (Psalm 115:16).
- The sun shall not smite by day, nor the moon by night (Psalm 121:6).
- Keep the city so that we won't watch in vain (Psalm 127:1). Cause us to speak with the enemies at the gate (Psalm 127:5).
- Deliver us from our enemies + we (flee) run to you to hide us (Psalm 143:9).
- Of they mercy cut off our enemies & destroy all that afflict our soul...we are your servants (Psalm 143:12).
- Strengthen the bars of our gates + make peace in our borders (Psalm 147:13-14).

Psalm 149:6-9
- High praise in our mouth + two-edged sword.
- To execute vengeance upon the heathen + punishments on the people.
- To bind their kings with chains + nobles with fetters of iron.
- To execute upon them the judgments written.
- THIS HONOR HAVE ALL HIS SAINTS, PRAISE YE THE LORD.

Prayer Devotionals #3:

Prayers that Shift Atmospheres

- Break up the fallow grounds; the unplowed grounds; the stony grounds (Jeremiah 4:3).
- Prepare the way in the wilderness (Isaiah 40:3).

- Make the highway straight in the dessert (Isaiah 40:3).
- Remove mountains, hindrance, limitations, blocks, barrier, and resistance (Isaiah 40:4).
- Bring the hills low, and exalt and lift up valleys (Isaiah 40:4).
- Make the crooked places straight and the rough places smooth (Isaiah 40:4).
- Pull down, destroy, and throw down demonic powers (Jeremiah 1:10).
- Bring down walls (Joshua 6:20).
- Pull down strongholds (2 Corinthians 10:4).
- Cut the bars of iron asunder (Psalm 107:16).
- Break the gates of brass (Psalm 107:16).
- Open prison doors (Isaiah 61:1).
- Cause us to possess gates of our enemy (Genesis 22:17).
- Activate the key of David. Open doors that no one can shut & shut doors that no one can open (Isaiah 22:22).
- Cause the wilderness to become a paradise (Isaiah 51:3).
- Cause the desert to become a garden (Isaiah 51:3).
- Cause the barren to become fruitful (Psalm 113:6,9.)
- Cause the desolate to become abundant (Isaiah 51:3).
- Strengthen Zion & comfort the waste places (Isaiah 51:3).
- Make pools in the wilderness + springs in dry land (Isaiah 41:18; Isaiah 35:6).
- Open rivers in high places + fountains in valleys + streams in deserts (Isaiah 41:18; Isaiah 35:6).
- Make waters from a rock (Psalms 78:16).

Luke 10:17
- Cause demonic principalities fall from heaven like

lightening.
- Shake demons off their thrones.
- Cripple demonic powers.
- Exploit powers of darkness.

- Shift the powers in the heavens (Haggai 2:6; Hebrews 12:26)

In Jesus's name, Amen.

Other Books by Jonathan Ferguson Include:

1) *Prophets 101*
2) *Experiencing God in the Supernatural Newly Revised: Prophetic Acceleration*
3) *Learning the Language of God*
4) *Wealth Zones: How to Locate Your Economic Zip Code*
5) *Jesus in HD (High Demand): Prophetic Insight into Revival & Evangelism*
6) *Advance: Emerging Apostles & Apostolic Centers*
7) *Secrets of Prophetic Accuracy*

And more to come...

Made in the USA
Middletown, DE
01 July 2017